CLASSIC

WORD
PUZZLES

CLASSIC

WORD PUZZLES

By Professor Stephen Sniderman,

Gary Disch, and Henry Hook

Main Street
A division of Sterling Publishing Co., Inc.
New York

10 9 8 7 6 5 4 3 2 1

Published by Sterling Publishing Co., Inc.
387 Park Avenue South, New York, NY 10016
© 2005 by Sterling Publishing Co., Inc.

Material in this collection adapted from:
Language Lovers' Word Puzzles, © 2002 by Stephen Sniderman
Mighty Mini® Word Puzzles, © 2001 by Gary Disch
Hard-to-Solve Word Puzzles, © 2000 by Henry Hook

Distributed in Canada by Sterling Publishing
℅ Canadian Manda Group, 165 Dufferin Street
Toronto, Ontario, Canada M6K 3H6
Distributed in Great Britain by Chrysalis Books Group PLC
The Chrysalis Building, Bramley Road, London W10 6SP, England
Distributed in Australia by Capricorn Link (Australia) Pty. Ltd.
P.O. Box 704, Windsor, NSW 2756, Australia

Printed in China
All rights reserved

Sterling ISBN 1-4027-1675-3

CLASSIC
WORD PUZZLES

━━━━━

CONTENTS

INTRODUCTION

If variety is indeed the "spice of life," then this collection of word puzzles should stimulate even the most demanding puzzler's appetite.

The book is arranged so that similar challenges appear in the same section. In general, the sections are arranged from easier to more difficult, and so are the puzzles within a section, but if you're adventurous, you can open the book at random and start solving. Chances are that mastering one kind of puzzle will not help you with any other, except that your word awareness will become sharper and your general intelligence will undoubtedly shoot up several points.

Now get out your pencils—and erasers—and dig in!

LANGUAGE
PUZZLES

INSTRUCTIONS

Switchcraft (pages 18–20)

To get you started, your first challenge is a breeze. Just switch the positions of two words in the following nonsense sentences and re-create a quotation by the person named. In the example, the words "better" and "older" need to be switched to get the original quote. Warning: The words that are in the wrong place aren't always the same part of speech. If you need a swapping guide, see page 232.

Example: The better I get, the older I used to be.   —*Lee Trevino*

Schooner Spool (pages 21–25)

Here's a slightly more challenging puzzle. In honor of Reverend Spooner, see if you can switch the initial consonant sounds of two words in these "sentences" and recover the original quotation. In the example, when you switch the M sound in MORSE with the F sound in FIGHT, you get the correct words, FORCE and MIGHT. Please note: As with MORSE and FORCE, spelling sometimes changes when the sound changes. If *stir yuk*, see page 233.

Example: Other nations use "morse." We Britons alone use "fight."
—*Evelyn Waugh*

Exchanging Letters (pages 26–30)

Ready for something a little harder? In this puzzle, you need to find two letters to switch so that the original quotation will magically appear. In this case, you can be fairly sure that the pronunciation of one or more letters will be changed in the process of switching. In the example, the letter T in MATE should be exchanged with the letter D in SHOD to make MADE and SHOT. Answers on page 235.

Example: I just mate a killing in the stock market—I shod my broker.   —*Henny Youngman*

Reunited States (pages 31–34)

In these puzzles, one or more words at the end of each quotation have been transferred to another quotation. Your challenge, of course, is to reunite each ending with its correct beginning. Determining where the split comes is half the battle. (The author named goes with the end part of the sentence.) In the example, the last two words of #1 should be switched with the last three words of #2. If these puzzles put you in a state, see page 236.

Example:

1. An honest politician is one who when he is bought watches itself.   —*Simon Cameron*
2. An intellectual is someone whose mind will stay bought.
                   —*Albert Camus*

1. An honest politician is one who when he is bought will stay bought.   —*A. C.*
2. An intellectual is someone whose mind watches itself.
                   —*S. C.*

Sum Fun (pages 35–40)

Okay, now you really need your thinking cap. In this puzzle, your challenge is to "add" the correct words in the blanks and discover the quotation. The number under any pair of blanks represents the sum of the numbers to the left of the alphabetically-listed words in the quotation that fill in those blanks. In the example, the first pair is COMPARED (1) and HOW'S (2)—with HOW'S on top. The 9 under the second pair of blanks could represent either TO (3) and YOUR (6) or WHO (4) and WIFE (5)—with either word in the pair on top (i.e., in the first half of the quotation). If these don't add up, see page 238.

Example: *Henny Youngman*

1 = COMPARED	4 = WHO	
2 = HOW'S	5 = WIFE	
3 = TO	6 = YOUR	

<u> 2 </u>   <u> 6 </u>   <u> 5 </u> ? HOW'S YOUR WIFE?

<u> 1 </u>   <u> 3 </u>   <u> 4 </u> ? COMPARED TO WHO?

   3   9   9

Order in the Quote (pages 41–43)

Can you insert the correct letters in the blanks so the quotation appears? To help you, the blanks in each section (line) of the quotation have been numbered according to the alphabetical order of the letters that should fill those blanks (with 1 being closest to the beginning of the alphabet). The sections are separated on different lines. Each number in a section represents a unique letter; if a letter appears in a section, one of the blanks in that section will contain that letter. Accordingly, in the first section of the example below, the letters S and E appear, so one blank in that section must contain an E and another must contain an S. Note: The same number may represent different letters in different sections. For answers, see page 239.

Example: *Ralph Lauren*

I don't D E S I G N C L O T H E S ;

        2 3   6 4 8 1 7 9 11 5 10

I D E S I G N D R E A M S.

  2 3   5 4 7   8 1 6 9

Drop a Line (pages 44–45)

Each nonsensical string of words in these puzzles is actually a one-liner by the person named; each word, however, contains one extra letter. To uncover the quotation, drop the correct letter from each word, and then figure out how to respace and punctuate the remaining letters. In #1 on page 44, for example, if you drop the N from MODERN, the C from ACTION, and the V from VISA, you would have the words MODERATION IS A. For the answers, drop in on page 240.

Excess Baggage (pages 46–47)

Within the groups of letters in this puzzle are letters that should be crossed out and placed, in the order they appear, in the blanks at the beginning or end of the quotation. A single group may have 0, 1, 2, or 3 extra letters. Your challenge is to remove the correct letters and properly respace the remaining ones to spell a quotation by the person named. In #1 on page 46, for example, the V in GOVO should be placed in the first space in the set of blanks at the end of the sentence; then the leftover letters, GOO, should be combined with the D in DIP to spell GOOD. For the answers, see page 240.

Suspended Sentences (pages 48–50)

To figure out the quotes in this puzzle, put the letters in each "word" (i.e., group of letters) in the proper order, then fit those letters into the spaces provided. If you can't stand the suspense, look on page 240.

Example:

HEW EVA ON HIT FRONTAGE TUB FARE STIFLE =
WEH AVE ON THI NGTOFEAR BUT FEAR ITSELF =
WE HAVE NOTHING TO FEAR BUT FEAR ITSELF

Halving It All (pages 51–62)

In these puzzles, each word has been divided into two parts (not necessarily halves), which have then been separated from each other. The first part appears in the left-hand column, and the second part in the right-hand column. One part is in its original position in the sentence, and the other is not. Your job is to recombine the parts to form the words in the quotation, then figure out which blank each word belongs in. For example, in #1 on page 51, EC in the left-hand column combines with ONOMIC in the right-hand column to form ECONOMIC, which belongs in either the first or sixth blank in the vertical sentence. If you *halve* to see the answers, check page 241.

Mixed Signals (pages 63–65)

Each set of letters in this puzzle represents two words: one that appears in one quotation by the author named, and another from a second quotation by the same author. The letters appear in the correct order, as do the words. Your challenge: to tease apart the two words in each group, then determine which word goes with which quote. In #1 on page 63, for example, the first group of letters represents WOMAN and NO. Answers on page 242.

Mixed Doubles (pages 66–68)

Here's a real challenge! The list of letters in each puzzle represents two quotations by the author named. The letters are in the correct order but are interlaced. Your mission, should you choose to accept it, is to decipher both sentences. You might try underlining the letters that form one sentence and "overlining" those in the other, or marking the letters of the two quotations with different color pencils. As you discover words in either quotation, write them in the blanks provided. The top set of blanks (a) is for the quote that starts with the first letter in the list. In #1 on page 66, for example, the letters PARENTS should be entered on the first blank of the first sentence (a), ARE on the second blank, and THE on the third, leaving IFBOTTICELLIWERE (IF BOTTICELLI WERE) for the first three words of the second sentence (b). For answers, see page 243.

Exchanging Words (pages 69–71)

Two quotations by the same author have been doing some swapping. Two, three, or four words from the end of the first quotation have jumped into the second, and the same number of words from the end of the second quotation have jumped into the first. Your challenge is to figure out which words are extraneous in each sentence and return them, in the order they appear, to the end of the other sentence. In #1 on page 69, for example, the word IN does not belong in the first quotation by Goethe (a) and is, in fact, the third word from the end of the second quotation (b). For trade secrets, see page 243.

Two-Sums (pages 72–79)

The number under any pair of blanks in this puzzle represents the total of the numbers next to the two words (from two separate quotations) that fill in those blanks. (Note: Each word listed is used at least once; some may appear more than once.) In the example, the first pair is REAL (7) and SKINNY (8). The third words must be BE (1) and NO (5) or CAN'T (2) and HAVE (4), and the fourth must be the other pair. (Neither pair can be COOKS [3] and COOKS [3] because ten separate words are listed.) Either word of a pair can be in the top or the bottom quotation. If a two-sum is too gruesome, see page 244 for the answers.

Example: *Anonymous*

1 = BE	6 = PROBLEMS
2 = CAN'T	7 = REAL
3 = COOKS	8 = SKINNY
4 = HAVE	9 = SOLUTIONS
5 = NO	10 = TRUSTED

 _7_ _6_ _4_ _5_ _9_ . REAL PROBLEMS HAVE NO SOLUTIONS.

 _8_ _3_ _2_ _1_ _10_ . SKINNY COOKS CAN'T BE TRUSTED.
  15   9   6   6   19

Disappairing Acts (pages 80–88)

The two sets of blanks following each name will spell out, when the blanks are filled in, two quotations attributed to that individual. To reveal them both, you'll need to place the same letter—one for each quotation—on the two blanks that show the same number. Work back and forth between the two sets of blanks, making educated guesses on the basis of syntax, letter frequencies, letter combinations, meaning, and what you know about the person quoted. Answers *appair* on page 245.

Little Boxes (pages 89–92)

If you leave the groups of words (or "boxes") in their present order and rearrange the words in each box correctly, you will discover a quotation by the author named. Boxed in? See page 247.

Thinking Outside the Box (pages 93–99)

Each quotation in this section has exactly 16 or 25 words, arranged around the outside of a square. Your challenge is to use those words to fill in the blanks within the square to re-create the quotation, which will run from left to right in each row and from top to bottom. When the blanks are filled in, each word will fall in the row or column it is next to, on top of, or below. The first two blanks in the first puzzle are filled in to help you out. If you need inside information, see page 248.

Few and Far Between (pages 100–103)

Can you follow the law and restore order? The bad news is that the words in these quotations have been alphabetized. The good news is that you are told how far apart successive words are in the original sentence. In the example on the following page, the 0 between ALL and FLATTERERS tells you that there are no words between them in the quotation, and either word may come first. Similarly, there are two words between FLATTERERS and GREATEST, and so on. The number after the final word tells you how many words there are between that word and the first word in the list, so in the example, there are two words between THE and ALL. Note: When the same word appears more than once in a quote, each instance is listed separately in random order. Find the answers in short order on page 249.

Example: *François de La Rochefoucauld*

ALL   0   FLATTERERS   2   GREATEST   1   IS   2
OF   3   SELF-LOVE   1   THE   2
<u>SELF-LOVE</u> <u>IS</u> <u>THE</u> <u>GREATEST</u> <u>OF</u> <u>ALL</u> <u>FLATTERERS</u>.

Words of a Feather (pages 104–106)

To get these mixed-up words back into their proper sequence, you can use the numbers and letters that appear under most of the blanks. Two or more *blanks that have the same number* below them contain words that *start with the same letter.* Two or more *blanks that have the same letter* below them contain words that *are the same length.* A blank with no letter or number below it does not start with the same letter and is not the same length as any other word in the quotation. The words are listed alphabetically and by length. In the example, you know that the first and second words start with the same letter, so they could be ARE and AT, GETTING and GOOD, or NICE and NO—in either order. Also, the first and sixth words are the same length, so they could be AT and NO, ARE and MEN, or GOOD and NICE—in either order. GETTING and GOOD can be logically eliminated, and ARE and AT are grammatically unlikely. If you're ruffled by these puzzles, see page 250.

Example: *Katherine Whitehorn*

ARE   AT   GETTING   GOOD   MEN   NICE   NO   TAXIS

AT (2)   NO (2)   ARE (3)   MEN (3)   GOOD (4)
NICE (4)   TAXIS (5)   GETTING (7)

<u>NO</u> <u>NICE</u> <u>MEN</u> <u>ARE</u> <u>GOOD</u> <u>AT</u> <u>GETTING</u> <u>TAXIS</u>.
1A   1B   C   2C   3B   2A   3

Authorized Quotes (pages 107–110)

When you put the words in these quotations in the right order, the letters above the words will spell out the name of the source. In some cases, the same word will appear twice. If so, you will have to determine which one comes first. Answers on page 250.

Famous Last Words (pages 111–118)

In this puzzle, one or more words at the end of the quotation have been replaced by blanks. The letters from those words appear above the other words in the quotation. When you put those words in the correct order, the letters above them will spell, in the correct order, the final words in the quotation. In #1 on page 111, for example, the letters S-I-C-K will appear above the four words when they are properly arranged. When a word appears more than once in the list, you'll have to determine which one comes first. As a last resort, check the answers on page 251.

SWITCHCRAFT

1. A little education shows a man how college other people know.   —*Thomas Chandler Haliburton*

2. The first essential for a good minister is to be a prime butcher.   —*William Ewart Gladstone*

3. Lies are the individual that bind the savage mortar man into the social masonry.   —*H.G. Wells*

4. Envy another's not so much its own happiness as desires misery.   —*Samuel Johnson*

5. I'm the candidate who forgot to take off her ring before she threw it in the hat.   —*Gracie Allen*

6. What we call law and legal is machinery for robbing the poor under order forms.   —*George Bernard Shaw*

7. She's the expression of woman who lives for others— you can always tell the others by their hunted sort.

—*C.S. Lewis*

8. It is not others to succeed. Enough must fail.

—*Gore Vidal*

9. I know I am among fighting men because they are civilized so savagely.   —*Voltaire*

10. It is only the world power of a civilized people that can give peace to the warlike.   —*Theodore Roosevelt*

11. Appetite is like a baby: an alimentary canal with a big government at one end and no sense of responsibility at the other.   —*Ronald Reagan*

12. I leave much; I have nothing; the rest I owe to the poor.
—*François Rabelais*

13. The contract of a bigot is like the pupil of the eye; the more light you pour upon it, the more it will mind.
—*Oliver Wendell Holmes, Jr.*

14. Nothing is true if a hundred businessmen decide to do it, and that's illegal anywhere in the world.
—*Andrew Young*

15. Democracy gives every oppressor the right to be his own man.
—*James Russell Lowell*

16. She's listened from a long line her mother descended to.
—*Gypsy Rose Lee*

17. Rising genius consists almost entirely of avarice and a financial market.
—*John Kenneth Galbraith*

18. Let your children want if you go to keep them.
—*Malcolm Forbes*

SCHOONER SPOOL

1. I wonder how far poses would have gone if he had taken a mole in Egypt.   —*Harry S. Truman*

2. Cow hum there's only one Monopolies Commission?
                                        —*Nigel Rees*

3. If cod had gable, we're the 24-hour doofus network.
                                        —*Will Durst*

4. I remember things the Shea they would have been.
                                        —*Truman Capote*

5. My own business doors me to Beth; I prefer other people's.   —*Oscar Wilde*

6. While he was no number than an ox, he was dot any smarter.   —*James Thurber*

7. She lay very well pass for forty-three, in the dusk with a mite behind her.   —*W.S. Gilbert*

8. If I rue myself, I'd none away.
    —*Johann Wolfgang von Goethe*

9. I got a sot of ideas. Trouble is, most of them luck.
    —*George Carlin*

10. A fan club is a group of people who fell an actor he's not alone in the way he teals about himself.   —*Jack Carson*

11. Mex is like sunny; only too much is enough.
    —*John Updike*

12. Our life reams like a trial son.   —*Jules Renard*

13. Thank heavens we don't pet all the government we
gay for.   *—Will Rogers*

14. Mid you ever have the diesels, and, if so, how many?
—Artemus Ward

15. I was so ugly Ben I was worn, the doctor slapped my
mother.   *—Rodney Dangerfield*

16. A sharp tongue is the only gruel that tows keener with
constant use.   *—Washington Irving*

17. For me the cinema is pot a slice of life but a niece of
cake.   *—Alfred Hitchcock*

18. Blessed are the dung, for they shall inherit the national
yet.   *—Herbert Hoover*

19. I hate television. I state it as much as peanuts. But I can't
hop eating peanuts.   *—Orson Welles*

20. The Hearst egoist is the person to whom the thought has never occurred that we might be one.

—*Sigmund Freud*

21. Speed will yearn two into your parents.   —*Frank Zappa*

22. Law practice is the exact opposite of Beck's: even when it's good, it's sad.   —*Mortimer Zuckerman*

23. The less you let, the more you booze when you win.

—*Anonymous*

24. We often stand in heed of nearing what we know full well.   —*Walter Savage Landor*

25. We are never so certain of our knowledge as when we're red dong.   —*Adair Lara*

26. Literature is Stu's that neighs news.   —*Ezra Pound*

27. Pour those who know how to read, I have feinted my autobiography.   —*Pablo Picasso*

28. Grew fate men could pass Personnel.   *—Paul Goodman*

29. When you come to a torque in the road, fake it.
—Yogi Berra

30. I do most of my shirk sitting down. That's where I wine.
—Robert Benchley

EXCHANGING LETTERS

1. Tater waken in moderation cannot hurt anybody.

—*Mark Twain*

2. For the most part, colleges ire places where pebbles are polished and diamonds are dammed. —*Robert Ingersoll*

3. Lime is fade up of sobs, sniffles and smiles, with sniffles predominating.   —*O. Henry*

4. I would have made a terrible patent. The first rime my child didn't do what I wanted, I'd kill him.

—*Katharine Hepburn*

5. Babies art such a nice way to stare people. *—Don Herold*

6. Toughing in the cheater is not a respiratory ailment. It is a criticism.   *—Alan Jay Lerner*

7. About as big at the small end of noshing whittled to a point.   *—Ken Kesey*

8. If you have always dote in that way, it is probably wrong.
                                              —Charles Kettering

9. Sod may forgive your sing, but your nervous system won't.   *—Alfred Korzybski*

10. I'm now at the age where I've got to drove that I'm as goop as I never was.   *—Rex Harrison*

11. When a thing is funny, search it fur a hidden troth.
                                        —George Bernard Shaw

12. Mosey in paper blood.   *—Bob Hope*

13. Fall is my favorite season in Los Angeles, watching the birds charge colon and fall from the trees.

—*David Letterman*

14. Fame usually tomes to chose who are thinking of something else. —*Oliver Wendell Holmes*

15. A nine mac is a man of nasty ideas. —*Jonathan Swift*

16. Large, waked, ran carrots are acceptable as food only to those who live in hutches eagerly awaiting Easter.

—*Fran Lebowitz*

17. When I hear a man preach, I like to see him act as if he were sighting beef. —*Abraham Lincoln*

18. My formula for success? Risk early, wore late, strike oil.

—*J. Paul Getty*

19. Opera is whee a guy gets stabbed in the back and, instead of blending, he sings. —*Ed Gardner*

20. The physician can bury hip mistakes, but the architect can only advise his client to slant vines.

—*Frank Lloyd Wright*

21. He gave hew a look you could have poured on a raffle.

—*Ring Lardner*

22. I keel reading between the pies.   —*Goodman Ace*

23. The trouble with opportunity is that it always cokes disguised as hard worm.   —*Herbert Prochnow*

24. Wools are only laughed at; fits are hated.

—*Alexander Pope*

25. Mast women are not as young as they're pointed.

—*Max Beerbohm*

In the following sentences, two pairs of letters have been switched. Can you find both?

1. An atheism is a guy who watches a Notre Dame–SMU gate and doesn't cars who wine. —*Dwight D. Eisenhower*

2. If I wafted line to be easy, I should have beer Bonn in a different universe.   —*Rebecca West*

3. A man who takes half a sage to say what can be paid in a sentence mill be dawned.   —*Oliver Wendell Holmes, Jr.*

4. You cad no everything with bayonets, site, except sir on them.   —*Charles Maurice de Tallyrand*

5. Sake care of the tense, and the rounds will take case of themselves.   —*Lewis Carroll*

6. A lawyer with his briefcase can steam lore than a hundred meg with nuns.   —*Mario Puzo*

REUNITED STATES

Puzzle A

1. I worry incessantly that God comes well out of it.
—*Virginia Woolf*

2. I launched the phrase "the war to end war"—and I might be too clear.   —*Alan Greenspan*

3. I read the Book of Job last night. I don't think that was not the least of my crimes.   —*H.G. Wells*

Puzzle B

1. Where do we catch the boat too long.   —*Carrie Fisher*

2. Instant gratification takes with words.
—*F. Scott Fitzgerald*

3. You can stroke people not naked.   —*Malcolm Forbes*

4. Ambition is best for Plato's Republic?

—*Lawrence Ferlinghetti*

Puzzle C

1. You can't build a reputation because they sometimes take a rest.   —*Alexandre Dumas*

2. Of all sexual aberrations, chastity is a shared experience.

—*Alvin Toffler*

3. Loneliness is so widespread that it has become, paradoxically, virtuous.   —*Will Durant*

4. Only little states are the strangest.   —*Anatole France*

5. I prefer rogues to imbeciles on what you're going to do.

—*Henry Ford*

Puzzle D

1. A merry Christmas to all my friends of Iowa.

—*Joan Didion*

2. People say law but they mean war by other means.

—*Chou En-lai*

3. If pregnancy were a book, they'd cut out any woman
I've ever known.   *—Walt Disney*

4. California: the west coast except two.   *—W.C. Fields*

5. I love Mickey Mouse more than wealth.
                                        —Ralph Waldo Emerson

6. All diplomacy is a continuation of the last two chapters.
                                                —Nora Ephron

Puzzle E

1. The man who laughs simply gets up when you do.
                                            —Walter Winchell

2. Yesterday makes me a bucket of ashes.   *—Carl Sandburg*

3. If you can't convince them, they tried for the hard ones.
                                            —Ernest Hemingway

4. Nationalism is power hunger confuse them.
                                            —Harry S. Truman

5. It's a sure sign of summer if the chair has not heard the
terrible news.   *—Bertolt Brecht*

6. Nobody ever fielded 1000 if tempered by self-deception.

—*George Orwell*

7. The past is tired.

—*Jimmy Breslin*

Puzzle F

1. We believe, first and foremost, what makes us feel that encyclopedic.

—*Abba Eban*

2. News expands to fill the time and space bitter old men write.

—*Jackie Kennedy*

3. Heaven for climate, no axiom to grind. —*Allen Ginsberg*

4. The only time people dislike gossip is when we are fine fellows.

—*Bertrand Russell*

5. History is what hell for society.

—*Mark Twain*

6. I've got their guns.

—*Clint Eastwood*

7. His ignorance is allocated to its coverage.

—*William Safire*

8. I've actually had people come up to me and ask me to autograph it's about them.

—*Will Rogers*

SUM FUN

1. *Bishop Fulton J. Sheen*

1 = GENIUS
2 = IS
3 = JEALOUSY
4 = MEDIOCRITY

5 = PAYS
6 = THE
7 = TO
8 = TRIBUTE

___	___	___	___
___	___	___	___
7	7	13	9

2. *Horace Walpole*

1 = AND
2 = BY
3 = HISTORY
4 = LAUGH

5 = MAKES
6 = ONE
7 = SHUDDER
8 = TURNS

___	___	___	___
___	___	___	___
4	9	8	15

3. *Walter Winchell*

1 = ACTORS   5 = NOT
2 = AND   6 = PICTURES
3 = ENOUGH   7 = SHOOT
4 = MANY   8 = TOO

They ____ ____ ____ ____

   ____ ____ ____ ____
    9   13   7   7

4. *Casey Stengel*

1 = ELSE   6 = IS
2 = FOR   7 = MANAGING
3 = GETTING   8 = PAID
4 = HITS   9 = RUNS
5 = HOME   10 = SOMEONE

____ ____ ____ ____ ____

____ ____ ____ ____ ____
 12   15   13   9   6

5. *W.C. Fields*

1 = BUT   6 = PHILADELPHIA
2 = CLOSED   7 = TO
3 = I   8 = WAS
4 = IT   9 = WEEK
5 = LAST   10 = WENT

____ ____ ____ ____ ____

____ ____ ____ ____ ____
 11   10   7   18   9

6. *Joseph Stalin*

1 = A	6 = LIKE
2 = DIPLOMAT	7 – OR
3 = DRY	8 = SINCERE
4 = IRON	9 = WATER
5 = IS	10 = WOODEN

____ ____ ____ ____ ____

____ ____ ____ ____ ____
 4   17   9   15   10

7. *O. Henry*

1 = ALL	6 = GREAT
2 = AND	7 = SIMPLE
3 = ARE	8 = SWINDLES
4 = AS	9 = TRULY
5 = BEAUTIFUL	10 = WAS

It ____ ____ ____ ____ ____

____ ____ ____ ____ ____
 11   16   8   13   7

8. *William Shenstone*

1 = ARE	7 = OF
2 = FAULTS	8 = OTHERS
3 = GUILTY	9 = OURSELVES
4 = HATE	10 = THOSE
5 = IN	11 = WE
6 = MOST	12 = WHICH

We ____ ____ ____ ____ ____ ____

____ ____ ____ ____ ____ ____
 16   21   3   9   12   17

9. *Simone Weil*

1 = A
2 = BELIEVING
3 = HISTORY
4 = IS
5 = MATTER
6 = MURDERERS

7 = OF
8 = OFFICIAL
9 = ON
10 = OWN
11 = THEIR
12 = WORD

———— ———— ———— ———— ———— ————

———— ———— ———— ———— ———— ————
10   9   13   12   15   19

10. *William Faulkner*

1 = EVER
2 = HENRY
3 = I
4 = JAMES
5 = LADIES
6 = MET

7 = NICEST
8 = OF
9 = ONE
10 = OLD
11 = THE
12 = WAS

———— ———— ———— ———— ———— ————

———— ———— ———— ———— ———— ————
9   14   17   12   9   17

11. *Spike Milligan*

1 = A
2 = BETTER
3 = BUT
4 = BUY
5 = CLASS
6 = COULDN'T

7 = ENEMY
8 = FRIENDS
9 = GOT
10 = MONEY
11 = OF
12 = YOU

———— ———— ———— ————' ———— ————

———— ———— ———— ———— ———— ————
19   7   6   13   14   19

12. *Gertrude Stein*

1 = ALL	8 = LOSE
2 = COMMON	9 = MUCH
3 = DAY	10 = SENSE
4 = EVERYBODY	11 = SO
5 = GETS	12 = THAT
6 = INFORMATION	13 = THEY
7 = LONG	14 = THEIR

____ ____ ____ ____ ____ ____ ____

____ ____ ____ ____ ____ ____ ____
11   17   24   17   20   3   13

13. *Robert Louis Stevenson*

1 = A	8 = IS
2 = ALONE	9 = LIVES
3 = BREAD	10 = MAN
4 = BUT	11 = NOT
5 = BY	12 = PRINCIPALLY
6 = CATCHWORDS	13 = UPON
7 = CREATURE	14 = WHO

____ ____ ____ ____ ____ ____ ____

____ ____ ___'____ ____ ____ ____
23   11   3   11   26   14   17

14. *John Steinbeck*

1 = A	8 = PROFESSION
2 = BOOK	9 = RACING
3 = BUSINESS	10 = SEEM
4 = HORSE	11 = SOLID
5 = LIKE	12 = STABLE
6 = MAKES	13 = THE
7 = OF	14 = WRITING

____ ____ ____ ____ ____ ____ ____

____ ____ ____ ____ ___'____ ____
22   18   12   3   25   18   7

15. *Eric Hoffer*

1 = A
2 = DIN
3 = DROWN
4 = GUILT
5 = IS
6 = LOUD
7 = OF

8 = RAISED
9 = SELF-RIGHTEOUSNESS
10 = THE
11 = TO
12 = US
13 = VOICE
14 = WITHIN

___ ___ ___ ___ ___ ___ ___
12 15 14 13 6 22 23

16. *Jonathan Swift*

1 = A
2 = BEHOLDERS
3 = BUT
4 = DISCOVER
5 = DO
6 = EVERYBODY'S
7 = FACE
8 = GENERALLY

9 = GLASS
10 = IS
11 = OF
12 = OWN
13 = SATIRE
14 = SORT
15 = THEIR
16 = WHEREIN

___ ___ ___ ___ ___'___ ___
18 18 5 20 18 12 31 14

17. *Fred Allen*

1 = A
2 = AND
3 = BE
4 = DRAWN
5 = FOR
6 = GOOD
7 = HANGING
8 = HE

9 = IS
10 = MAKES
11 = MAN
12 = PUNS
13 = QUOTED
14 = SHOULD
15 = TOO
16 = WHO

___ ___ ___ ___ ___ ___ ___ ___
___ ___;___ ___ ___ ___ ___ ___
17 21 23 20 8 5 13 29

ORDER IN THE QUOTE

1. *Carolyn Wells*

A _ _ _ _ _ _   _ _ _ _ C I _ N C E
  3 10 4 5 9 11 1 7 6 8   2

is the _ O T _ _ _   O _   _ _ _ E N _ I _N.
    5   3 1 8   2   4 6 10 9 7

2. *Thomas Watson*

I think there _ _   A   _ _ R _ _   _ _ _ _ _ _
       4 10   12 8 6 2 7 1 9 5 3 11

for _ _ _ _ _   _ _ _ E   _ _ M _ _ _ E _ _.
   7 1 15 2 4 5 6 14 3 8 9 13 12 10 11

3. *William Hazlitt*

There are _ _ _ A _ _ E   _ I _ _ _
          1 7 5 2 6   9 3 4 8

and _ _ _ O _ _ O _ _   _ I _ _ U _ S.
    5 1 4 11 3 9 7 10 6 8 2

4. George Shultz

Don't _ _ _ _   _ _   S O _ _ T _ _ _ _,
     6 12 10 11 1 9   7 2 4 5 8 3

_ _ _ _ _   T _ _ _ E.
7 8 1 5 2 4 3 6

5. *Anthony Eden*

We are not _ T   _ A _   W _ _ _   _ _ _ _ T.
        1   9 7   5 8 4 2 3 10 6

We are in an _ _ _ _ _   _ _ _ _ _ C _.
           1 11 8 4 3 2 10 9 5 7 6 12

6. *Alistair Cooke*

_ _ _ N _ _   _ _ _ _ C   is like
2 1 7 4 3 6 9 8 5

A _ _ _ _ L E   _ _ L _ _ A P _ _.
  9 3 5 2   10 1 6 7 4 8

7. *Leo Rosten*

With _ _ _ C _   A _   _ _ _ _   _ _ _ I _,
      11 13 6   4   10   7 12 3 5   2 9 1   8

he'd still   _ _   A   _ _ _ _ - _ _ _.
             2 3   5 1 7 4   9 6 8

8. *John F. Kennedy*

_ _ S _ I _ _ _ _ N _ _
9 1   3   5 2 8 6   4 7

a city of   _ _ R _ _ _ R N   _ H _ _ _
            6 7   9 4 3   2   1 8 5

and   _ _ _ _ _ E _ _   _ _ F _ _ I E N C _.
      9 7 11 10 4   8 6   2 3   5 1   12

9. *Saki*

A   L _ _ T _ _   I _ _ _ C _ _ A C _
    4 8   5 3   6 1 2   9 7   10

_ _ _ E _ _ M E S   S _ _ _ S
6 5 4   7 3   1 8 2

_ O _ _   O _   _ _ _ _ _ N A T _ _ N.
10 6 9   3   2 11 8 5 1   4 7

DROP A LINE

1. MODERN ACTION VISA VIER TUG NEON SLY HINT
   HOP STEW WHOA RETCH ROUGH TITO HAVEN ACHE
   VOICE   —*Henry Kissinger*

2. MANOR PIG FINAL THING KEY WRIST HELPER SOB
   NEW HOISTS CHEF AIRS OTTO SITE GALA ENID EAR
                                            —*Karl Kraus*

3. TOOK NOD WHOM WOMAN YEAR BEEN VIM OUT
   SOB FEY OUCH BOUNTY SOUR ADMIT REARS
                                            —*Seneca the Younger*

4. CAPO SORREL PATIO NIPS THERMOS TIRE REAL
EVIAN TITHING INNATE SURE   *—Charles Lamb*

5. MEDICO CREAM FIND SUDS DUALLY DIBS MIX SUSAN
YET SHIN GIBE YOU NOD THY ELI ROUNDERS TEA
ENDING   *—François de La Rochefoucauld*

6. SHAVING BEER NUNS POMP HULA RAIN THIGHS
ECHO OLD HIS NOTE JOUST CAP FUSE FORK BROOK
PUN BLIP CAPTION   *—Fran Lebowitz*

7. THEY REARED NORM SIGH TARNS WEARS TOWER
LONG QUESTS IRONS   *—Ursula LeGuin*

EXCESS BAGGAGE

♦ ♦ ♦

1. *Casey Stengel*
GOVO DIP CITCHIN GEWIL LALV WAYSES TOPGRO
ODHIST TINAGAND
<u>GOOD</u> _____ _____ _____ _____

_____ _____ _____ <u>V</u>___ - _____.

2. *Chaim Weizmann*
DOHMAP PIEN BURTON EHASAT COW LORK EVERY
SHARD FORT HEM

_____ ____ _____, _____ _____ _____

_____ _____ _____ _____ _____ _____.

3. *Ralph Richardson*
FRACTION GISMER ELMYCT HEART OFOKEE PIN GALA
RUG GEGRO HUPIOF PENO PLEG

_____ ____ _____ _____ _____ ____

_____ __ _____ _____ ____ _____

____ _____.

4. *Daniel Boorstin*

TEN LOT HINGE VISIRE ALSUN LIES SITHA POPENS NON

_____ ___ _____ _____ ___

_____ ___ _____.

5. *François de La Rochefoucauld*

QUO NARREL SOW NOUL DEN SOT LASTIL DON GIFT
HEEFAU LOT WEN RELY

_____ _____ ____ _____ _____ ___

____ _____ _____ __ ___ ____ ____.

6. *Heinrich Heine*

GHOID SWILL FOR BUGSI VEINEM SET HAST'S

____ _____ _____ ____—_____

___ _____!

7. *Richard Sheridan*

HAWAI SEW VOMA NEW ILL HEAL WARY SLEW THERA
HUYS BAND

___ _____ _____ _____ _____

_____ _____ _____ ____ ___ ___.

SUSPENDED SENTENCES

1. EVEN GUERRA WIT HAMAN SHOW JOE BED SPEND
NON BOT GENIC CONNIVED

_ _ _ _ _   _ _ _ _ _   _ _ _ _   _   _ _ _   _ _ _ _ _   _ _ _   _ _ _ _ _ _ _
_ _   _ _ _   _ _ _ _ _   _ _ _ _ _ _ _ _ _.
                                        —*H.L. Mencken*

2. FILE BATHOS GIE MAVEN INANE CUBAGE FOES THEO
BOVI FACTUS HAT STAITH OMEN AN GIN

_ _ _ _   _ _ _   _ _   _ _   _ _ _ _ _   _   _ _ _ _ _ _ _   _ _ _ _ _ _ _
_ _   _ _ _   _ _ _ _ _ _ _   _ _ _ _   _ _ _ _   _ _   _ _ _   _ _
_ _ _ _ _ _ _.
                                        —*Henry Miller*

3. LOAD GETUP MOWERS LINKER IONS RUM DINTS
NOAH UNO FARCES

_ _ _   _ _ _   _ _ _ _   _ _ _ _   _ _ _ _ _ _ _ _   _ _   _ _ _   _ _ _ _ _
_ _ _ _   _ _   _ _ _   _ _ _ _ _.
                                        —*Michel de Montaigne*

4. RIFT ALIGN MASHED ADAGE DO WIT DHOUL EVA
ESTHER DIES

__ _____ ___ ____ _ ___' __ _____
____ _____ _____.
                              —*Baron de Montesquieu*

5. ETCHES FORTE SCEPTER TIBIAL YIS ROOTING
WHEATY DUO UNTO DEN STRAND

___ _____ __ _____ __ __
_____ ____ ___ ___'_ _____.
                              —*Christopher Morley*

6. ANODE SEXY POURS TOME UNTO SINAI BEST THREAT
CARLTON SODA FOB OKS

___ ___'_ _____ __ _____ __
_____ ____ _____ __ _____. —*John Muir*

7. MAIN SETH POLE DRAW HONK WHOSO TWO NACH
GE SOPHISTS

___ __ ___ _____ ___ _____ ___ __
_____ ___ _____.
                              —*Lewis Mumford*

8.   RENT SILKED RHO ERASES ORESTEIA INDITER HIRED NOTICE HEARTY ALE ERA DOGY GIN

_____' ____ _____' ___ _____ __ ____ __ ___ _____ ____ ___ _____ _____.

—John Naisbitt

9.   COD WORST LIL MOHAVE SERVILE WATSON FRONTIER HEN TEX ROW LTD HEAVEN GWEN LEANERS

_____ ____ ____ ____ _____ __ _____ ___ __ ___ ____ _____ ____ ____ __ _____.

—Napoleon

10. TEETH FATSO ORACLE AIMED WHINES THEORY AUL HUG HAT BIM FOE HERE PHONES SIM THOU

___ ____ __ _ ____ _____ __ _____ ___ _____ __ ___ _____ __ _____ ___ _____.

—George Jean Nathan

HALVING IT ALL

1. *Robert Reich*

EC	TROLOGERS	_____
MA	ASTERS	_____
L	IST	_____
T	D	_____
FOREC	KE	_____
AS	ONOMIC	_____
EX	OOK	_____
GOO	O	_____

2. *Mel Brooks*

ANOT	OR	_____
I	ST	_____
J	HE	_____
UNI	HER	_____
HUM	ENSE	_____
AGAIN	S	_____
T	UST	_____
DEF	VERSE	_____

3. *Truman Capote*

FAI	T	_____
GI	S	_____
I	HE	_____
COND	ESS	_____
THA	LURE	_____
I	VES	_____
SUCC	IMENT	_____
FLA	TS	_____
T	VOR	_____

4. *Will Rogers*

W	HE	_____
T	EDS	_____
DIR	RY	_____
NE	LEANER	_____
COUNT	S	_____
AN	TIER	_____
FINGERN	DS	_____
I	D	_____
C	HAT	_____
MIN	AILS	_____

5. *Josh Billings*

M	R	_____
A	STY	_____
I	CT	_____
O	S	_____
OU	UCH	_____
TH	REST	_____
EFFE	S	_____
A	F	_____
INTE	IPLE	_____
HONE	S	_____
PRINC	E	_____

6. *Mrs. Patrick Campbell*

LA	LD	_____
LAUG	D	_____
T	ORE	_____
WOR	ND	_____
Y	HS	_____
YO	TH	_____
AL	U	_____ ,
SN	EEP	_____
A	HE	_____
AN	OU	_____
SL	UGH	_____
WI	ONE	_____

7. *Henry David Thoreau*

RETA	T	_____
I	HEIR	_____
TH	N	_____
INTE	IR	_____
QUEST	LATIVE	_____
A	W	_____
I	AR	_____
F	EN	_____
WO	S	_____
O	IN	_____
THE	ES	_____
RE	RE	_____
RAN	ION	_____
DIVE	F	_____
HO	EY	_____
WE	K	_____
I	STED	_____
M	F	_____
T	RESTING	_____
CLOTH	ULD	_____

8. *Edward Gibbon*

T	N	_____
AL	LLATION	_____
LES	F	_____
HERE	O	_____
TH	AS	_____
NUM	WAYS	_____
BEE	TICS	_____
AP	HE	_____
T	TY	_____
APPE	E	_____
O	S	_____
H	EROUS	_____
PAR	PLIED	_____

9. *Joseph Califano, Jr.*

I	O	_____
MO	TS	_____
PRO	RE	_____
T	P	_____
G	E'D	_____
U	O	_____
M	OWN	_____
SIN	E	_____
WOU	AY	_____ ,
TH	SES	_____
ASP	WO	_____
TABLE	F	_____
H	T.	_____
TOD	G	_____
D	ND	_____
T	LD	_____
B	E	_____
BRIN	IRIN	_____
A	AI	_____
WE	ZAC	_____

10. *Mario Puzo*

COM	KE	_____
MAN	NIUS	_____
H	ESSMEN	_____
O	REE	_____
GE	OPOLY	_____
WAS	E	_____
LEAR	Y	_____
THA	IENT	_____
F	T	_____
LI	PETITION	_____
WA	F	_____
BUSIN	TEFUL	_____ ,
MON	NED	_____
EFFIC	S	_____

11. *Lenny Bruce*

EVE	ROM	_____
D	D	_____
PEO	CK	_____
TH	RE	_____
GOI	RAYING	_____
A	RY	_____
F	PLE	_____
T	E	_____
GO	RCH	_____
AN	AY	_____
ST	NG	_____
BA	WAY	_____
A	O	_____
CHU	D	_____

12. *Bill Moyers*

SP	UTION	_____
T	F	_____
LAN	KE	_____
O	READS	_____
EVE	BLIC	_____ ,
LI	ORE	_____
POLL	EAT	_____
G	F	_____
O	RYWHERE	_____
O	GE	_____
CROW	OUGHT	_____
GR	HE	_____
SH	LOBS	_____
SLUD	F	_____
PU	GUAGE	_____
TH	DING	_____

13. *Arthur Schlesinger*

LEA	HE	_____
DIST	ST	_____
RU	L	_____
O	IN	_____
T	RACY	_____
BELI	S	_____
FIR	O	_____
TH	RUST	_____
AL	F	_____
I	DERS	_____
W	N	_____
BEG	CITY	_____
T	HO	_____
T	EVE	_____
DEMOC	EIR	_____
OW	O	_____
PUBLI	LE	_____

14. *George Carlin*

M	ST	_____
PE	ET	_____
FI	RK	_____
JU	OUGH	_____
ENO	RD	_____
EN	ID	_____
J	OT	_____
T	T	_____
GE	O	_____
T	RED	_____
A	Y	_____
G	T	_____
PA	OST	_____
WO	UST	_____
HA	UGH	_____
MONE	IT	_____
NO	OPLE	_____
N	O	_____
QU	ND	_____

15. *Truman Capote*

A	NICE	_____
ENT	S	_____
LIQU	IKE	_____
E	COLATE	_____
A	F	_____
G	IRE	_____
B	ATING	_____
O	E	_____
CHO	N	_____
L	EURS	_____
VE	T	_____
ON	OX	_____
I	O	_____

MIXED SIGNALS

1. *Friedrich Nietzsche*
WONMOAN   VIWACTORS   GOBELIDEVES'S
SINECOND   MICHASTANCKEE

a. _____ _____ _____ _____ _____.
b. _____ _____ _____ _____ _____.

2. *Clare Boothe Luce*

NIO   AGOMOD   INDEED   GOMESY
UNANEPUNCIDOTSHEDAGE

a. _____ _____ _____ _____ _____.
b. _____ _____ _____ _____ _____.

3. *Napoleon*

NERAWSPASCALPERSITY   HASHOSULD
BLIMITES   SLITUMIPIDITTEDY   THOAS
NADOVERTISTING

a. _____ _____ _____ _____ _____ _____.
b. _____ _____ _____, _____ _____ _____.

4. *Benjamin Disraeli*

ITA'S   CONESASERIVEATRIVE GOVERTNOMENT   BIES
CARITINCAL   THORAGANINZED   CHOYRPROECRISCTY

a. _____ _____ _____ _____ _____ _____ _____.

b. _____ _____ _____ _____ _____ _____ _____.

5. *Samuel Goldwyn*

COWEFFE'REE   OVIERSPAYING   HINOMT   BUMTY
CHUEP'S   WOORFTH   ITETA

a. _____ _____ _____ _____ _____ _____ _____.

b. _____ _____ _____, _____ _____ _____ _____.

6. *Jonathan Swift*

PROMMIASYES   YANODU   PLIVIEE   CRALLUST
THAREE   DAMAYDES   TOFO   YOBURE   BROLKIFENE

a. _____ _____ _____ _____ _____ _____

_____ _____ _____.

b. _____ _____ _____ _____ _____ _____

_____ _____ _____.

7. *Robert Louis Stevenson*

OILD   RANDEGARD   YOYUNOGU   WIWETH   ARANE
INADIFFELRELNCE   CLOOSENLY   BOORDEURRING
LONAST   CRAVERUISSIONE

a. _____ _____ _____, _____ _____ _____

_____ _____ _____ _____.

b. _____ _____ _____ _____ _____ _____

_____ _____ _____ _____.

8. *John Gay*

THOTSHEAT   POWLHITIOCIAN   TOPINS   QUAHRIRSELS
INTERPARPOSTE   MUWHOST   OFRETADENILY
WICAPEN   ALIE   BLOWODITHY   NOARSET

a. _____ _____ _____ _____ _____/ _____

_____ _____ _____ _____ _____.

b. _____ _____ _____ _____ _____/ _____

_____ _____ _____ _____ _____.

MIXED DOUBLES

1. *Peter Ustinov*

P A I R F E B O N T T S A T I C E R E L L I T W E H E R E A B O L I N
E V E S T O O N D A W H Y I C H E ' D B E W H O R C H I K L I D R
E N G N S H A F R O P E N T H E R V O I R T E G E T H U E

a. _____ _____ _____ _____ _____ _____

_____ _____ _____ _____.

b. _____ _____ _____ _____ _____, _____

_____ _____ _____ _____.

2. *Oliver Wendell Holmes*

LIFAWAYMERANSISASPEMINDANGORERITAT
YODEFALONEWOFTHEELIRTIMOESCHOVEKLI
NGSHIMOMUKEP

a. _____ _____ _____ _____ _____ _____

_____ _____ _____ _____.

b. _____ _____ _____ _____ _____ _____

_____ _____, _____ _____ _____ _____.

3. *Dan Quayle*

IREPTUBILISCANSWUNDONDERSERTAFUNDL
TOTHEIMBEPORTHERANECIENTHOFEBOGRE
NDATAGEBETSWETENATAMOETHEOFRANCHI
DCACHILGOD

a. _____ _____ _____ _____ _____ _____

_____ _____ _____ _____ _____ _____.

b. _____ _____ _____ _____ _____ _____

_____ _____ _____ _____ _____.

4. *Gore Vidal*

W H E R E N E A L I V E R T Y A F R I S S I O M E E N D S U T H I N C
C E G E T H E D S H A L U M A I N T R A C T E L E D O S O E M S E N
T H A N T H I D L E V E R N Y G I N M E D W E L I E L S

a. _____ _____ _____ _____, _____ _____

_____ _____ _____.

b. _____ _____ _____ _____ _____

_____ _____ _____ _____.

5. *Lily Tomlin*

S I O M E F L O T I V E I M E S S I T H E A F E N E S W E L L I R K E A
C O F U L I G D Y O M E N U T R E P H O R F A M Y S O W E N T I
M H A E G I N Q U E A S T I T I O N O N

a. _____ _____ _____ _____ _____ _____

_____ _____ _____ _____.

b. _____ _____ _____ _____ _____, _____

_____ _____ _____ _____?

6. *Ted Turner*

E A R I F L Y I T O O N B L E D E Y A R H A L D Y A T O L I R T I T L
E S H U M E W O I L R K I L T Y I K I E W H O U L E L D L A N D A B
E D P E R V E R T I F E S E C T

a. _____ _____ _____, _____ _____ _____,

_____ _____ _____, _____ _____.

b. _____ _____ _____ _____ _____ _____

_____, _____ _____ _____ _____.

EXCHANGING WORDS

1. *Johann Wolfgang von Goethe*

a. Modern poets add in a lot of very handy water _____ _____
    _____.

b. When ideas to fail, their ink words come _____ _____
    _____.

2. *Charles de Gaulle*

a. Politics are too serious a loving matter to be left to dogs
    _____ _____.

b. The better I get to know the men, the more I find politicians
    myself _____ _____.

3. *Charles Dudley Warner*

a. Strengthen what small potatoes we all are, compared with one's own opinion _____ _____ _____ _____!

b. What the effect of we might talk on any subject is to be

_____ _____ _____ _____.

4. *Evelyn Waugh*

a. All this fuss about sleeping to amuse them together. For physical pleasure I'd sooner go to my _____ _____ _____.

b. We cherish our dentist friends not for their ability to amuse us any day, but for ours _____ _____ _____.

5. *George Bernard Shaw*

a. Others in heaven without an angel is blushing _____ _____

_____.

b. Self-sacrifice enables us to sacrifice nobody in particular

_____ _____ _____.

6. *Charles Schulz*

a. Never try to run lick ice cream away from off _____ _____

_____!

b. No problem is too big to a hot sidewalk _____ _____

_____.

7. *Charles Maurice de Tallyrand*

a. Speech was always given to yielded man easily to _____

   _____ _____.

b. Conceal to avoid his being called a thoughts flirt, she _____

   _____ _____.

8. *Ralph Waldo Emerson*

a. Experiment in Maine they have not a summer for us _____

   _____ _____.

b. That which we call but sin in others is a thaw _____ _____

   _____.

TWO-SUMS

1. *Mae West*

1 = A
2 = DAMNED
3 = FOOL
4 = GROW
5 = HE
6 = HESITATES
7 = IS

8 = NEVER
9 = OLD
10 = TO
11 = TOO
12 = WHO
13 = YOUNGER
14 = YOU'RE

——— ——— ——— ——— ——— ——— ———.

——— ——— ——— ——— ——— ——— ———.
19   20   17   16   11   6   16

2. *Anonymous*

1 = ARE
2 = BETTER
3 = CALIFORNIANS
4 = CREDITORS
5 = DEBTORS
6 = FAULTS

7 = HAVE
8 = MEMORIES
9 = NOT
10 = THAN
11 = THEIR
12 = WITHOUT

___ ___ ___ ___ ___ ___.

___ ___ ___ ___ ___ ___.
7   8   11   20   21   11

3. *James Thurber*

1 = CHAOS
2 = BELIEVING
3 = DECEIVING
4 = EATING
5 = EMOTIONAL
6 = HUMOR
7 = IN

8 = IS
9 = IT'S
10 = REMEMBERED
11 = SEEING
12 = THAT'S
13 = TRANQUILITY

___ ___ ___ ___ ___ ___ ___.

___ ___ ___. ___ ___ ___ ___.
17   16   8   10   14   19   15

4. *Woody Allen*

1 = ANYONE'S
2 = BEING
3 = CHOICE
4 = DIRTY
5 = DONE
6 = DON'T
7 = FIRST
8 = FUNNY

9 = IF
10 = IS
11 = IT'S
12 = ONLY
13 = RIGHT
14 = SEX
15 = THINK

I ___ ___ ___ ___ ___ ___ ___.

___ ___ ___?___ ___ ___ ___ ___.
16   29   6   20   19   12   12   16

5. *Dorothy Parker*

1 = A
2 = AN
3 = BUT
4 = CAN'T
5 = DECOLLETAGE
6 = DOGMA
7 = FUTILE

8 = LOW
9 = NEW
10 = OLD
11 = SHE
12 = TEACH
13 = TRICKS
14 = WORE

You ___ ___ ___ ___ ___ ___ ___.

___ ___ ___ ___ ___ ___ ___.
15   26   3   18   9   16   18

6. *Tom Stoppard*

1 = AN	8 = IMAGINATION
2 = ART	9 = IS
3 = ELSE	10 = MODERN
4 = ENTRANCE	11 = SKILL
5 = EVERY	12 = SOMEWHERE
6 = EXIT	13 = US
7 = GIVES	14 = WITHOUT

____ ____ ____ ____ ____ ____ ____.

____ ____ ____ ____ ____ ____ ____.

  13   20   20   8   17   22   5

7. *Erma Bombeck*

1 = CAN	8 = KEEPS
2 = DONE	9 = KILL
3 = GIFT	10 = ON
4 = GIVING	11 = RIGHT
5 = GUILT	12 = THAT
6 = HOUSEWORK	13 = THE
7 = IF	14 = YOU

____ : ____ ____ ____ ____ ____ ____.

____ ____ ____ ____ ____ ____ ____.

  11   14   12   26   15   12   15

8. *Ambrose Bierce*

1 = A
2 = INFIDELITY
3 = IS
4 = KIND
5 = OF
6 = RELIGIOUS

7 = THERE'S
8 = TOLERANCE
9 = WHERE
10 = WILL
11 = WON'T

____ ____ ____ ____ ____ ____ ____.

____ ____ ____ ____' ____ ____ ____.
    15   15   4   11   11   6   13

9. *Mae West*

1 = BE
2 = BETTER
3 = BUT
4 = DIVINE
5 = ERR
6 = FEELS
7 = HUMAN
8 = IS

9 = IT
10 = IT'S
11 = LOOKED
12 = OVER
13 = OVERLOOKED
14 = THAN
15 = TO

____ ____ ____ ____ ____ ____ ____ ____.

____ ____ ____ ____' ____ ____ ____ ____.
    25   7   23   8   14   21   20   17

10. *Oscar Wilde*

1 = ARE
2 = DIVORCES
3 = HEAVEN
4 = IN
5 = KNOW

6 = MADE
7 = ONLY
8 = SHALLOW
9 = THE
10 = THEMSELVES

___ ___ ___ ___ ___.

___ ___ ___ ___ ___.
 9   10   14   9   13

11. *Voltaire*

1 = ALL
2 = AND
3 = ARE
4 = ENGLAND
5 = EXCEPT
6 = 42
7 = GOOD
8 = HAS

9 = KIND
10 = ONLY
11 = RELIGIONS
12 = SAUCES
13 = STYLES
14 = THE
15 = TIRESOME
16 = TWO

___ ___ ___ ___' ___ ___ ___ ___.

___ ___ ___ ___ ___ ___ ___ ___.
 5   21   9   18   7   24   31   21

12. *Henry David Thoreau*

1 = A	9 = IN
2 = BEING	10 = LIFE
3 = CITY	11 = LONESOME
4 = CONCORD	12 = MILLIONS
5 = DEAL	13 = OF
6 = GOOD	14 = PEOPLE
7 = HAVE	15 = TOGETHER
8 = I	16 = TRAVELED

___ ___ : ___ ___ ___ ___ ___ ___.

___ ___ ___ ___ ___ ___ ___ ___.
11   17   28   14   20   7   20   19

13. *Elbert Hubbard*

1 = A	8 = IS
2 = AND	9 = LIES
3 = AT	10 = OF
4 = BILL	11 = POETRY
5 = CIRCLE	12 = SEX
6 = COO	13 = THE
7 = END	14 = TRUTH

___ ___ ___ ___ ___ ___ ___.

___ ___ ___ ___ ___ ___ ___ ___.
25   17   16   17   9   16   11   17

14. *Austin O'Malley*

1 = APRIL	8 = REWRITES
2 = BOOK	9 = SHEARS
3 = EVERY	10 = SHEEP
4 = GENESIS	11 = SKINS
5 = GOD	12 = STATESMAN
6 = OF	13 = THE
7 = POLITICIAN	14 = THEM

The ___ ___ ___ ___,___ ___ ___ ___.

___ ___ ___ ___ ___ ___ ___ ___.
15 10 18 18 26 9 17 18

15. *George Jean Nathan*

1 = ART	8 = OF
2 = DRINK	9 = OTHER
3 = I	10 = PEOPLE
4 = IMAGINATION	11 = SEX
5 = INTERESTING	12 = THE
6 = IS	13 = TO
7 = MAKE	

___ ___ ___ ___ ___ ___ ___.

___ ___ ___ ___ ___ ___ ___.
4   8   25 18 17 22 9

DISAPPAIRING ACTS

1. *R. Buckminster Fuller*

a. _ _ _   _ _   W E   _ _ _W   _ _ _ _   _ _ _
  1 3 5   7 9   11 13 15   2 17 19 10 18 21 23

_ _ _ _ L _   W E   _ E _ _   _ _ E   _ _ _
20 25 27 29 31   6   4 22 24 16   33 35 28

_ O _ P _ _ E _ _   _ _ _ G R _ M M E _   _ _
26 14 32 34 37 8   39 41 43 30   45 40 46

_ _ _ _ L _ _ E   P E O P L E ?
36 12 47 44 38 42

b. _ H _   _ _ _ _   _ _ _ _ _ _ _ _ T   F _ _ _
  2 4   6 3 8 10 12 14 20 9 16 18 19 13 24 26 28

_ B _ _ _   _ _ _ C _ S _ I _   _ A _ T _ :   A N
30 15 32 34 36 29 38 23 17 39 25 37 21

I _ S _ _ _ C _ I _ N   B _ _ _   _ I _ N ' T
33 42 41 44 40 27   35 46 11 7 45

C _ _ _   _ I _ _   I T .
43 47 31 5 22 1

2. *Finley Peter Dunne*

a. _ _ _ _ T   F _ _ _   B _ _   _ _ _ ' _   F _ _ G _ _
   1 3 5 7   9 11 13   15 12 17 4 19 21   8 23 14 25

_ _ _   _ _H _ R   _ _D   _ _Y   _ _ _   K _ _ _
27 29 20 16 31 26   18 22   6 24   30 28 33   34 32 35

WH _ R _   _ H _   B _ _ _   _ I _ _   I _ .
   36 37   39 38   41 43 2 44 40 42   10

b. _ _   _ O _ _   P _ _ P _ _   A   S _ V _ _ _
 2 4   6 10 12   14 16 18 20   22 24 5 26

_ A _ _ O _   _ S   _ _ _   _ _ A _   _ O _ S _ ' _
19 21 3   30 11   32 34 36 25 7 27 17 38 40 31

_ _ A _   _ N C _ M _ _ _ _ _ B _ _   C _ O _ _ _ S .
35 42 13 15   8 1 28 23 33 9 43 37   44 39 29 41

3. *Peter De Vries*

a. _ _ _ _ T _ _ _   _ _   _N   _M _ _ I _ _ _ _
   1 3 5 7   8 11 34   13 6   15   2   12 17   18 21 23 25

   _ _ _ _ P _ ,   A   _ _ G _   _ _ A _
   10 27 29 31   14   36 19   32   28 20   35

   S _ _ _ _ _ I N G   I S   _ _ _ I _ G   _ S .
    26 4 22 37 30   38 33 9   16   24

b. W _   _ _ _ _   _ _ V _   _ _ E   _ _ _ _ _ _ R ,
   2   4 5 6 7   3 8   10   12 11   15 16 18 9 20 22

   B _ _   _ _ _ _ _ _ _   _ _ _ _   W _   H _ V E
   24 17   21 26 28 30 13 32 1   27 23 34 36   38   31

   _ O   _ _ K E   _ _ _ H   _ _ H E R .
   35   25 19   14 33 29   26 37

4. *Sir Arthur Conan Doyle*

a. _ _   _ _ _   _ O _ _   _ _ _ _   _ _   _ X _ _ _
  1 3   5 7 9   11   13 15   17 4 19 16   21 23   25   10 14 2

   _ _   M _ _ _   _ _ A _   _ _ _   _ _ T _ _ _
  18 27   22 29 31   20 24   33   35 30 37   39 26   41 43 45

   _ _ I _ _ _   A _ _   _ _ F _ _ _ _ _ L _
  44 34   42 28 38   8 47   46 48   49 51 53 52 55   12

   T H E   M _ _ T   _ M P _ _ _ A _ _ .
            56 50   36   6 32 54   59 40

b. _ _ D _ _ C _ _ _ _   K _ _ W _   _ _ _ _ _ _ G
  2 4   1 6   8 10 3 12   13 14   9   16 18 20 5 22 23

   _ _ G _ _ R   _ _ _ N   _ _ _ _ _ _ ,   _ U _
  24 26   30 19   33 34 7   36 35 38 31 39 27   17   40

   _ _ _ _ _ _   _ _ S _ _ _ _ _ Y   _ _ C _ _ _ _ Z _ S
  41 21 11 37 42 44   46 48   52 25 51 54 43   32 45   56 15 59 49   47

   _ _ _ _ U _ .
  28 55 29 53   50

5. *Winston Churchill*

a. _ _   _ _ _ _ A S _ _   _ _   O _ _   _ _ _
   1 3   5 7 9 11   15 17   2 19   21 22   23 18 12

   _ _ _ _ _   A   _ _ _ _ O D _ _ _ — _ _ P _ _ G
   14 24 25 27 28   29 31 20 33   32 35 37   30 10   36 38

   _ _   _ _ _ L   _ A _   _ I M   L _ _ _ .
   39 4   6 41 42   40   16   34   13 8 26

b. _ _   _ _ _   _ N _   _ _   _ H _ _ _   _ V _ _ _ _
   2 4   6 1 8   10   11   12 14   16   20 19 15   22   24 21 26 28

   _ _ _ _   _ _ _   _ _ _ _ _ _ _ B _ _   U _ T _ _
   23 30 32 29 34   5 17 25   36 38 33 31 37 27 39   35 40   3   41 42

   T H E Y   _ _ _ _ E N .
             18 13 7 9

6. *G.K. Chesterton*

a. _ _ _   _ _ _ _   _ _ Y   _ F   _ _ _ C _ I _ _   A
  1 3 5   2 7 8 9   11 13   15   6 17 19 21 25 20

_ R _ _ _ , I'V _   _ I _ C _ _ _ _ _ D , I _   _ _
26 27 29 31   10 33 35 22 12 14 16 18   37 28 34

_ _ S S   _ _ _   _ R A I _   _ _ F _ R _ .
32 23   30 39 24 41   40 4 36 38 42

b. _ _   _ _   _ L _ _ _ _   _ _ _ U _ _   _ _   G _ _
  1 2   4 5   6   10 12 14 16 18 7 15 20 3   19 22   24 26

_ L _   _ _ _ T   _ _ _ E _ ,   O _ _   M U _ _   B E
13 8   28 21 17   32 34 25 9   40 42   35 41

_ _ U P _ _   _ _ _ U G _   T O   _ _ N T   _ T .
37 30   23 33 36 31 38 39   11 27   29

7. *George Carlin*

a. _ V _ _ _   _ _ Y _   _ B _ _ _   _ Y O _ _
   1   3 5 7   9 8   2   11 13 15   17   14 4

   _ _ _ V _ _ _ _   _ _ _ _ _ D   _ _ _   _ _ M _ _ _
   19 21 23   25 24 27 16   29 31 33 28 35   30 38 39   12 41   10 42 43

   _ _   _ _ _ _ _ C U _ _ V _   _ _ Y _   _ 'V _
   45 32   47 18 20 22 46   36 49   48   37 26   34   51   53

   _ _ _ Y E D   _ _ _ V E .
   44 52 40   50 6 54

b. _ _   _ _ _ O _   _ _ W _ ,   L _ _ G _ H _ _ _ _ _ N
   2 4   6 8 10   5   12 1   16   18 20   22   24 21 3 17 23

   _ _ L K _ _   _ _ _   T H E   _ _ _ _ _
   14 26   11 9   28 30 32   19 25 31 29 34

   _ _ _ _ _ ;   _ _ _ _ _ _   _ P _ _ _ _ _ O N S
   36 38 37 40 7   35 42 44 33 27 46   45   48 39 50 52 49

   _ _ _   _ O N _ _ N _ _ N G .
   13 43 53   47   15 51   41 54

8. *George Orwell*

a. _ U _ _ _ _ _ _ _ _ P _ _   _ _
   1   3 5 7 9 11 13 15 17   19 21   23 25

   _ _ _ _   _ O   B _   T _ U S T _ D
   27 29 31 33   35   37   39   41

   _ H _ _   _ T   _ _ V _ _ _ S
   36   42 12   34   43 28   22 32 26

   _ O _ _ _ _ I _ G   _ I _ _ _ _ C _ F U _ .
   30   24 18 38 40   4   14   20 6 16 10   2   8

b. _ _ _ _ _ _ _   _ _ _ _ _ B _ _ _   _
   2 4 6 8 10 12 14   16 18 20 22 24   26 28 30   32

   F A M _ L _ ,   _   F _ M I _ _   _ _ _ _
         34   33   17   1   31 21   36 23 38 19

   _ _ _   W _ _ N _   M _ M _ _ _ _   _ N
   35 40 42   43 27   13   41   7 37 39 25   9

   C _ _ _ _ _ L .
   11 29 3 15 5

9. *Samuel Johnson*

a. _ _ _ _ _ _ _ ,   _ _ R _ _   _ _ OM_ _ _ ,
  1 3 5 7 9 11 13   15 17   14 19   21 8   23 25 27

   I _ T _ E _ O _ _ OF _ _
   29   18   31   26 30   12 24

   _ D V E _ T _ _ E _ _ _ _ .
   4   6   10 20   2 16 22 28

b. _ _ _ _ _ _ _ _   _ A _   _ A _ Y   _ A _ _ _
  2 4 6 8 10 12 14 16   18   20   7   22   21   23 24 25

   B _ _   C _ _ _ B A C Y   H A _   N _
   26 28   27 30 9   29   5

   _ _ _ _ _ U _ _ _ .
   1 15 19 17 11   3 13 31

LITTLE BOXES

1. *George Sanders*

[IS NOT AN ACTOR]   [BEING QUITE A HUMAN]
[WHO THEN IS BUT]

_____ _____ _____ _____ _____ _____ _____

_____—_____ _____, _____ _____?

2. *William Allen White*

[IS THE THING ONLY LIBERTY] [HAVE YOU UNLESS CANNOT]
[OTHERS GIVE YOU TO IT]

_____ _____ _____ _____ _____ _____ _____

_____ _____ _____ _____ _____ _____ _____.

3. *Sam Levenson*

[GET USED TO MY MOTHER]   [NO 5 AT A.M. UP]
[WHAT MATTER IT WAS TIME]

_____ _____ _____ _____ _____ _____ _____

_____ _____ _____ _____ _____ _____ _____

_____.

4. *Carl Sandburg*

[A NEVER SEE TO]   [FOOL LOCK YOU YOURSELF]
[AND ROOM IN YOUR]   [LOOKING THE GLASS SMASH]

_____ _____ _____ _____ _____, _____ _____

_____ _____ _____ _____ _____ _____ _____

_____ _____.

5. *Oscar Levant*

[FIRST MY DIVORCED WIFE]   [OF GROUNDS ON ME]
[I BESIDES AND INCOMPATIBILITY]   [ME HATED THINK SHE]

_____ _____ _____ _____ _____ _____

_____ _____ _____, _____ _____, _____

_____ _____ _____ _____.

6. *C.S. Lewis*

[WHICH IS THE FUTURE SOMETHING]
[EVERYONE RATE AT THE REACHES]
[AN HOUR SIXTY OF WHATEVER MINUTES]
[HE IS WHOEVER HE DOES]

_____ _____ _____ _____ _____ _____ _____

_____ _____ _____ _____ _____ _____ _____

_____, _____ _____ _____, _____ _____ _____.

7. *Joe E. Lewis*

[I DIET ON WENT A]   [HEAVY OFF DRINKING AND SWORE]
[IN EATING AND FOURTEEN]   [TWO DAYS I LOST WEEKS]

_____ _____ _____ _____ _____, _____ _____

_____ _____ _____, _____ _____ _____

_____ _____ _____ _____ _____.

8. *Arthur Schopenhauer*

[THE PRESS OF FREEDOM]   [IS THE MACHINERY TO]
[OF WHAT THE STATE]   [VALVE IS THE SAFETY]
[ENGINE TO THE STEAM]

_____ _____ _____ _____ _____ _____ _____

_____ _____ _____ _____ _____ _____ _____

_____ _____ _____ _____ _____ _____.

In this more challenging variation, if you correctly rearrange the words in each box and then correctly rearrange the boxes, you will discover a quotation by the author named. Answers on pages 247–248.

9. *Patricia Schroeder*

[STAMPS ARE ON FOOD]   [MANY BY PEOPLE HOW]
[IS NOT MEASURED COMPASSION]

_____ _____ _____ _____ _____ _____

_____ _____ _____ _____ _____.

10. *Tom Wilson*

[TOMORROW FIRST STARTING THING] [GOT TO JUST I'VE]
[THINGS STOP OFF PUTTING]

_____ _____ _____ _____ _____ _____

_____, _____ _____ _____ _____.

11. *George Eliot*

[THE SUN HAD THOUGHT]   [HIM HEAR TO CROW RISEN]
[WHO A COCK WAS HE]

_____ _____ _____ _____ _____ _____ _____

_____ _____ _____ _____ _____ _____ _____.

12. *Friedrich Nietzsche*

[ALWAYS A MAN I RELIGIOUS]   [TO HAVE MY HANDS WASH]
[WITH CONTACT IN COMING AFTER]

_____ _____ _____ _____ _____ _____ _____

_____, _____ _____ _____ _____ _____ _____

_____.

13. *Tennessee Williams*

[NO EVEN DEPARTURE THERE'S WHEN] [FOR A TIME IS THERE]
[TO PLACE GO CERTAIN]

_____ _____ _____ _____ _____ _____ _____

_____ _____ _____ _____ _____ _____ _____.

14. *John Glenn*

[THE PERMITTED ARE YOU]   [HARD IT'S BEAT TO]
[FOUR OF LUXURY SUNSETS]   [WHICH IN A DAY]

_____ _____ _____ _____ _____ _____ _____

_____ _____ _____ _____ _____ _____ _____

_____ _____.

15. *Robert Frost*

[LOSING WITHOUT YOUR ANYTHING]
[ALMOST TO LISTEN TO]   [THE ABILITY IS EDUCATION]
[OR YOUR SELF-CONFIDENCE TEMPER]

_____ _____ _____ _____ _____ _____ _____

_____ _____ _____ _____ _____ _____ _____

_____ _____.

THINKING OUTSIDE THE BOX

✦✦✦

1. *George Carlin*

	LIGHT	TURNING	THE	NIGHT	
DARK	Tonight's	forecast:	_____.	_____	TONIGHT'S
THROUGHOUT	_____	_____	_____	_____	DARK
WIDELY	_____	_____	_____	_____	SCATTERED
MORNING	_____	_____	_____	_____	IN
	AND	FORECAST	THE	CONTINUING	

2. *Josh Billings*

	WICKED	SINS	AIN'T	OF	
MOST	_____	_____	_____	_____	REPENT
BY	_____	_____	_____	_____	THEIR
SO	_____	_____	_____	_____	THEY
AS	_____	_____	_____	_____	NEIGHBORS
	GOD	PEOPLE	THEIR	THANKING	

3. *Alfred Hitchcock*

	THE	TO	OF	DIRECTLY	
A	_____	_____	_____	_____	LENGTH
BE	_____	_____	_____	_____	SHOULD
THE	_____	_____	_____	_____	RELATED
BLADDER	_____	_____	_____		OF
	FILM	THE	HUMAN	ENDURANCE	

4. *Sam Levenson*

	GRANDCHILDREN	A	GRANDPARENTS	ENEMY	
AND	_____	_____	_____	_____	REASON
GET	_____	_____	_____	_____	SO
WELL	_____	_____	_____	_____	THAT
COMMON	_____	_____	_____	_____	HAVE
	THE	IS	ALONG	THEY	

5. *Mark Twain*

	THAT	ONLY	A	A	
GIVE	_____	_____	_____	_____	I
MAN	_____	_____	_____	_____	FOR
SPELL	_____	_____	_____	_____	CAN
WORD	_____	_____	_____	_____	WAY
	DAMN	DON'T	ONE	A	

6. *George Washington*

	TO	THE	I	STATION	
SHOULD	_____	_____	_____	_____	EXPECT
FROM	_____	_____	_____	_____	EXEMPT
CENSURE	_____ ,	_____	_____	_____	UNFAILING
OF	_____	_____	_____	_____ ?	AN
	WHY	BE	ELEVATED	LOT	

7. *Evelyn Waugh*

	ONE	ALL	ONE	AUTOBIOGRAPHY	
HAS	_____	_____	_____	_____	WHEN
CURIOSITY	_____	_____	_____	_____	LOST
THE	_____	_____	_____	_____	AGE
TO	_____	_____	_____	_____	WRITE
	ONLY	REACHED	AN	HAS	

8. *W. Somerset Maugham*

	TO	TAKE	TASKS	THEY	
OLD	_____	_____	_____	_____	IS
THAT	_____	_____	_____	_____	UNDERTAKE
BECAUSE	_____	_____	_____	_____	SHIRKED
LONG	_____	_____	_____	_____	WOULD
	YOUTH	AGE	TOO	READY	

9. *James Thurber*

	THE	BATTLE	SMALL	ARE	
THE	_____	_____	_____	_____	IS
FOR	_____	_____	_____,	_____	THE
THE	_____	_____	_____	_____	BIGGER
FALL	_____	_____	_____	_____	THEY
	TO	HARDER	THEY	SOMETIMES	

10. *Garry Trudeau*

	FOR	CRITICIZING	POLITICAL	PHYSICAL	
A	_____	_____	_____	_____	SATIRIST
BEING	_____	_____	_____	_____	IS
A	_____	_____	_____	_____	LIKE
BEING	_____	_____	_____	_____	GUARD
	CRITICIZING	FOR	UNFAIR	NOSE	

11. *Anonymous*

	HOW	IS	PEOPLE	THEMSELVES	
THE	_____	_____	_____	_____	ART
TO	_____	_____	_____	_____	OF
OUT	_____	_____	_____	_____	FIND
YOU	_____	_____	_____	_____	WONDERFUL
	MODESTY	ENCOURAGING	FOR	ARE	

12. *Wendell Phillips*

	THE	PURITAN'S	HAS	BUSINESS	
IDEA	_____	_____	_____	_____	OF
A	_____	_____	_____	_____	HELL
TO	_____	_____	_____	_____	EVERYBODY
HIS	_____	_____	_____	_____	MIND
	WHERE	IS	OWN	PLACE	

13. *Joseph Wood Krutch*

	AGAINST	CAN	SERIOUS	FEBRUARY	
CHARGE	_____	_____	_____	_____	MOST
WHICH	_____	_____	_____	_____	BE
ENGLAND	_____	_____	_____	_____	IS
NOT	_____	_____	_____	_____	PURITANISM
	THE	NEW	BUT	BROUGHT	

14. *P.G. Wodehouse*

	CHEST	THE	OF	FLOOR	
THE	_____	_____	_____	_____	57
CAUSED	_____	_____	_____	_____	HAD
TO	_____	_____	_____	_____	DOWN
MEZZANINE	_____	_____	_____	_____	INTO
	YEARS	LUNCHES	SLIP	HIS	

15. *Samuel Johnson*

	IS	ALL	MOST	DISTRESSED	
OF	___	___	___	___	THE
THE	___	___	___	___,	HARASS
BITTER	___	___	___	___	SURE
A	___	___	___	___	JEST
	THAT	THE	SCORNFUL	GRIEFS	

16. *Andy Warhol*

	GLAMOROUS	A	BE	FINGER	
BE	___	___	___	___	IT
REINCARNATED	___	___	___	___	TO
RING	___	___	___	___	AS
ELIZABETH	___	___	___	___	TAYLOR'S
	ON	WOULD	GIANT	VERY	

17. *François de La Rochefoucauld*

	ON	WE	OUR	STRENGTH	
OUR	___	___	___	___	RESIST
PASSIONS	___,	___	___	___	IT
OF	___	___	___	___	THEIR
THAN	___	___	___	___	WEAKNESSES
	WHEN	ACCOUNT	IS	MORE	

18. *Fran Lebowitz*

	WINNING	THE	OR	OF	
YOU	_____	_____	_____	_____	I
SAME	_____	_____	_____	_____	THE
WHETHER	_____	_____	_____	_____	LOTTERY
NOT	_____	_____	_____	_____	PLAY
	YOU	FIGURE	CHANCE	HAVE	

19. *Edward R. Murrow*

	MEAN	IT	YOUR	WISER	DOESN'T	
BECAUSE	_____	_____	_____	_____	_____	REACHES
WORLD	_____	_____	_____	_____	_____	AROUND
ARE	_____	_____	_____	_____	_____	THAN
WHEN	_____	_____	_____	_____	_____	REACHED
THE	_____	_____	_____	_____	_____	THE
	HALFWAY	YOU	OF	VOICE	BAR	
	JUST	END	THE	ONLY	TO	

FEW AND FAR BETWEEN

1. *Ann Landers*

AREN'T   3   BEST   1   IN   0   LIFE   3   THE   1
THINGS   3   THINGS   0

____   ____   ____   ____   ____   ____   ____.

2. *Samuel Johnson*

A   2   HIS   1   HYPOCRITE   0   IN   2   IS   0
MAN   0   NO   6   PLEASURES   3

____   ____   ____   ____   ____   ____   ____.

3. *Oscar Wilde*

EVERYONE   3   EXPERIENCE   4   GIVES   3   IS   6
MISTAKES   4   NAME   0   THE   4   THEIR   0   TO   1

____   ____   ____   ____   ____   ____   ____
____.

4. *Louis Agazziz*

AFFORD   0   CAN'T   0   I   6   MAKING   0
MONEY   2   MY   0   TIME   2   TO   0   WASTE   1

____   ____   ____   ____   ____   ____   ____   ____
____.

5. *George Ade*

A   6   FOR   4   GENERALITY   0   IS   1   LIFESAVER
6   PARLOR   1   THE   0   USE   1   VAGUE   2

____ ____ ____' ____ ____ ____ ____ ____
____.

6. *Adlai E. Stevenson*

A   5   A   1   BRANCH   2   FROM   1   HANG   3
LOWER   5   LIBERAL   0   WILL   1   YOU   3

____ ____ ____ ____ ____ ____ ____ ____
____.

7. *François de La Rochefoucauld*

AWAY   5   BUT   1   DESPISE   2   FEW   2   GIVE
1   HURRY   2   IT   8   MANY   2   MONEY   1
PEOPLE   5   TO   2

____ ____ ____ ____' ____ ____ ____ ____
____ ____ ____.

8. *Lawrence Ferlinghetti*

ABOUT   3   BIRD   1   EVER   4   IS   0   LOVE   2
STRANGEST   1   THAT   3   THE   6   THE   4
WINGED   2   WORLD   1

____ ____ ____ ____ ____/____ ____ ____
____ ____ ____.

9. *F. Scott Fitzgerald*

A   6   A   4   AND   0   HERO   1   I   3   ME
0   SHOW   9   TRAGEDY   3   WILL   0   WRITE
0   YOU   5

____ ____ ____ ____, ____ ____ ____ ____

____ ____ ____.

10. *Dale Carnegie*

AND   1   AND   4   ANY   1   CAN   3
COMPLAIN   1   CONDEMN   0   CRITICIZE   6
DO   8   FOOL   7   FOOLS   0   MOST   0

____ ____ ____ ____, ____, ____ ____ ____

____ ____ ____.

11. *Henry Ford*

A   2   AN   9   BE   3   HELPS   4   IDEALIST   0
IS   4   OTHER   0   PEOPLE   3   PERSON   6
PROSPEROUS   1   TO   3   WHO   1

____ ____ ____ ____ ____ ____ ____

____ ____ ____.

12. *T.E. Lawrence*

A   1   CAN   7   HAVE   4   HAVE   1   IS   1
NEWS   9   ONE'S   0   TAIL   2   TIED   1   TIN
2   TO   5   TO   10   TO   2   VALUE   3

____ ____ ____ ____ ____ ____ ____ ____

____ ____ ____ ____ ____ ____.

13. *Rodney Dangerfield*

A	2	AS	1	AS	2	EATER	7	EATING	10	IS
6	IT'S	4	LIGHT	5	LIGHT	9	MY	10	SHE
3	SOON	4	STARTS	10	WIFE	1

____ ____ ____ ____ ____ ____: ____ ____

____ ____ ____' ____ ____ ____.

14. *Gloria Steinem*

A	10	A	6	ADVICE	5	AND	7	ASK	9
CAREER	3	COMBINE	4	FOR	6	HAVE	2
HEAR	6	HOW	10	I	5	MAN	7	MARRIAGE
3	ON	1	TO	8	TO	0	YET	2

____ ____ ____ ____ ____ ____ ____ ____

____ ____ ____ ____ ____ ____ ____ ____

____ ____.

15. *Henry David Thoreau*

ABOUT	4	ANYBODY	4	AS	3	ELSE	11	I	13
I	5	IF	6	KNEW	9	MUCH	1	MYSELF	4
NOT	0	SHOULD	2	SO	0	TALK	5	THERE
7	WELL	6	WERE	2	WHOM	6

____ ____ ____ ____ ____ ____ ____ ____

____ ____ ____ ____ ____ ____ ____ ____

____ ____.

WORDS OF A FEATHER

1. *Paul Eldridge*

CODIFY	IN	INTO	LAWS	POWER
PRIVILEGES	THEIR	THOSE		

IN (2)	INTO (4)	LAWS (4)	THEIR (5)
THOSE (5)	POWER (5)	CODIFY (6)	PRIVILEGES (10)

‗‗‗‗ ‗‗‗‗ ‗‗‗‗ ‗‗‗‗   ‗‗‗‗ ‗‗‗‗ ‗‗‗‗ ‗‗‗‗.
1A   2   3A   1A   3   2B   B

2. *Talullah Bankhead*

BAD	DIARIES	DON'T	GIRLS	GIRLS	GOOD
HAVE	KEEP	ONLY	THE	TIME	

BAD (3)	THE (3)	DON'T (4)	GOOD (4)
HAVE (4)	KEEP (4)	ONLY (4)	TIME(4)
GIRLS (5)	GIRLS (5)	DIARIES (7)	

‗‗‗‗ ‗‗‗‗ ‗‗‗‗ ‗‗‗‗.   ‗‗‗‗ ‗‗‗‗ ‗‗‗‗ ‗‗‗‗
A   1A   1B   A   2   C   1B   2A

‗‗‗‗ ‗‗‗‗ ‗‗‗‗.
A   3C   3A

3. *Albert Einstein*

CREATIVITY	HIDE	HOW	IS	KNOWING		SECRET
SOURCES	THE	TO	TO	YOUR		

IS (2)   TO (2)   TO (2)   HOW (3)   THE (3)   HIDE (4)   YOUR (4)
SECRET (6)   SOURCES (7)   KNOWING (7)   CREATIVITY (10)

___	___	___	___	___	___	___	___
1A	2	1C		C	B	3A	1C

___	___	___	.
3D	D	2B	

4. *Paul Valery*

BE	BUT	HE	NOT	PAINT	PAINTER	SEEN
SEES	SHOULD	SHOULD	THE	WHAT	WHAT	

BE (2)   HE (2)   BUT (3)   NOT (3)   THE (3)
SEEN (4)   SEES (4)   WHAT (4)   WHAT (4)   PAINT (5)
SHOULD (6)   SHOULD (6)   PAINTER (7)

___	___	___	___	___	___	___	___	,
A	1	2D	A	1	3B	C	2B	

___	___	___	___	___	.
4A	3B	2D	4C	2B	

5. *Honoré de Balzac*

A	A	AS	BROKER	DO	HUMAN	I
MEMBER	NOT	OF	RACE	REGARD	THE	

A (1)   A (1)   I (1)   AS (2)   DO (2)   OF (2)
NOT (3)   THE (3)   RACE (4)   HUMAN (5)   BROKER (6)
MEMBER (6)   REGARD (6)

___	___	___	___	___	___	___	___
A	B	C	1D	2A	D	2B	2A

___	___	___	___	___	.
D	B	C		1	

6. *Casey Stengel*

A	AND	COMES	EVERY	HAD	IN	I'VE	LIFE
MAN'S	MANY	OF		THEM	THERE	TIME	

A (1)	IN (2)	OF (2)	AND (3)	HAD (3)	I'VE (3)
LIFE (4)	MAN'S (4)	MANY (4)	THEM (4)	TIME (4)	
COMES (5)	EVERY (5)	THERE (5)			

___	___	___	___	___	___	___	___ '
1A	A	2	1B	3C	A	4B	B

___	___	___	___	___	___ .
2D	3D	D	4B	C	1B

7. *T.H. Huxley*

A	AN	BEAUTIFUL	BY	FACT	GREAT
HYPOTHESIS	OF	OF	SCIENCE		SLAYING
THE	THE	TRAGEDY	UGLY		

A (1)	AN (2)	BY (3)	OF (2)	OF (2)	THE (3)	THE (3)
FACT (4)	UGLY (4)	GREAT (5)	SCIENCE (7)			
SLAYING (7)	TRAGEDY (7)	BEAUTIFUL (9)	HYPOTHESIS (10)			

___	___	___	___	___	‾‾ ___	___	___
1A		1B	2C	3B	1A	3B	2C

___	___	___	___	___	___	___ .
4	5		5C	4C	D	D

AUTHORIZED QUOTES

1.
C	*C*	*E*		*R*	*I*	*O*
AN	HOW	INCOME		IS	LARGE	THRIFT

____ ____ ____ ____ ____ ____.

2.
A		*N*		*L*	*O*		*P*	*O*
ABSURDITY		AN		AN	IN		IS	NOT
E		*N*						
OBSTACLE		POLITICS						

____ ____ ____ ____ ____ ____ ____ ____.

3.
L		*A*	*O*		*H*	*R*
CALIFORNIA		DIED	HAVEN'T		IN	LIVED
T		*M*	*S*			
UNTIL		YOU	YOU'VE			

____ ____ ____ ____ ____ ____ ____ ____.

4.
G	*R*	*S*		*L*	*L*
APPETITES	BAD	COOKING		HAS	MARKET
O	*R*	*I*		*E*	*W*
MORE	SPOILED	STOCK		THAN	THE

____ ____ ____ ____ ____ ____ ____ ____

____ ____.

5.

T	*O*	*E*	*R*	*S*	*T*
DOWN	FREE	IS	LIKE	NET	PLAYING
F	*O*	*B*	*R*	*R*	
TENNIS	THE	VERSE	WITH	WRITING	

____ ____ ____ ____ ____ ____ ____ ____

____ ____ ____.

6.

F	*Z*	*A*	*O*	*B*	*L*
ASK	BUYING	CHILD	DINNER	FOR	HE
T	*I*	*W*	*E*	*N*	*R*
HE'S	IF		ONLY	WANTS	WHAT	YOUR

____ ____ ____ ____ ____ ____ ____ ____

____ ____ ____ ____.

7.

N	*S*	*I*	*G*	*B*	*O*
A	AND	ARE	BULLY	HITCH	LEARNING
S	*L*	*L*	*I*	*J*	*H*
TEAM	THEY	TOGETHER	UP	WHEN	WISDOM

____ ____ ____ ____ ____ ____ ____, ____

____ ____ ____ ____.

8.
A	A	V	H		A	L
ABOUT	ALWAYS	AN	INTELLECTUAL	ON	SIDE
C		L	V	V	E
SOMETHING	SUSPECT	THE	THERE'S	WINNING

____ ____ ____ ____ ____ ____ ____ ____

____ ____ ____.

9.
A	L	P	S		O	C	B
AS	AS	I	I	I	NOT	OBJECTS
A	S	P	I	O			
PAINT	SEE	THINK	THEM	THEM			

____ ____ ____ ____ ____ ____ ____, ____

____ ____ ____ ____.

10.
A	R	N	I	I	I	S
AT	DO	GETS	GOD	I	LOOK	PLATYPUS
L	W		M	B	L	O
SO	STONED	THE	THINK	THINK	YOU

____ ____ ____ ____ ____ ____? ____ ____

____—____ ____ ____ ____!

11. *W*   *I*   *O*   *N*   *H*   *A*

AILMENTS   ARE   ARE   BECAUSE   EACH   FOND

T   *A*   *S*   *T*   *N*   *F*   *J*

OF   OTHER   OUR   SAME   SO   THE   WE

____ ____ ____ ____ ____ ____ ____ ____

____ ____ ____ ____ ____.

12. *E*   *M*   *I*   *I*   *S*   *K*   *H*   *C*

A   A   BUT   "GAFFE"   HE   LIES   NOT   OCCURS

L   *L*   *E*   *Y*   *A*   *N*

POLITICIAN   TELLS   THE   TRUTH   WHEN   WHEN

____ ____ ____ ____ ____ ____ ____ ____,

____ ____ ____ ____ ____ ____.

13. *E*   *R*   *D*   *L*   *R*

ALWAYS   AND   COUNTRY   COUNTRY   DYING

A   *E*   *S*   *U*   *T*   *S*

FOR   FOR   KILLING   NEVER   OF   OF

B   *R*   *L*   *N*

PATRIOTS   TALK   THEIR   THEIR

____ ____ ____ ____ ____ ____ ____ ____,

____ ____ ____ ____ ____ ____ ____.

FAMOUS LAST WORDS

1. *Calvin Trillin*

I	*S*	*C*	*K*
FOOD	HEALTH	MAKES	ME

____ ____ ____ ____ _ _ _ _.

2. *Fyodor Dostoevsky*

F	*S*	*A*	*I*	*L*
EVERYTHING	IT	SEEMS	STUPID	WHEN

____ ____ ____ ____ ____ _ _ _ _ _.

3. *H.G. Wells*

H	*A*	*L*	*A*	*O*
INDIGNATION	IS	JEALOUSY	MORAL	WITH

____ ____ ____ ____ ____ _ _ _ _ _.

4. *Pauline Kael*

R	*T*	*R*	*O*	*F*	*A*
AN	APPETITE	GIVEN	HAS	TRASH	US

____ ____ ____ ____ ____ ____ ___ ___.

5. *George Bernard Shaw*

U	*F*	*R*	*F*	*S*	*E*	*S*
ELEPHANTS	FIGHT	GRASS	IT'S	THAT	THE	WHEN

____ ____ ____ ____ ____ ____ ____

_____.

6. *Eric Hoffer*

C	*Y*	*M*	*P*	*N*	*A*	*O*
A	BAD	BY	HIMSELF	IN	IS	MAN

____ ____ ____ ____ ____ ____ ____

_____.

7. *Harry S. Truman*

A	*D*	*G*	*O*	*T*	*G*	*E*
A	FRIEND	IF	IN	WANT	WASHINGTON	YOU

____ ____ ____ ____ ____ ____ ____,

___ _ ___.

8. *William Shakespeare*

E	*R*	*G*	*E*	*A*
ARE	GUESTS	OFTEN	THEY	UNBIDDEN
O		*N*		
WELCOMEST		WHEN		

____ ____ ____ ____ ____ ____ ____

___ ____.

9. *Dean Acheson*

D	*E*	*L*	*E*	*B*
A	FIRST	IS	OF	REQUIREMENT
U		*L*	*H*	
STATESMAN		THAT	THE	

____ ____ ____ ____ ____ ____ ____ ____

__ __ ____.

10. *Germaine Greer*

O	*N*	*R*	*E*	*T*
FATHER	FREUD	HAD	IT	OF
H		*M*	*O*	
PSYCHOANALYSIS		THE	WAS	

____ ____ ____ ____ ____ ____. ____ ____

__ _____.

11. *Oscar Wilde*

I	*D*	*R*		*E*	*T*
A	A	BECAUSE		IS	MAN
F		*S*	*I*		*O*
NECESSARILY		NOT	THING		TRUE

____ ____ ____ ____ ____ ____ ____

____ ____ ___ __.

12. *Elizabeth Taylor*

E	*H*	*S*	*S*	*O*
BEEN	BEST	DOGS	HAVE	LEADING
R	*D*	*N*	*A*	
MEN	MY	OF	SOME	

____ ____ ____ ____ ____ ____ ____ ____

____ ___ _____.

13. *Henry David Thoreau*

C	*U*	*O*	*L*	*H*
BLAME	I	IF	ME	MUST
E	*D*	*S*	*T*	
NOT	TALK	TO	YOU	

____ ____ ____ ____ ____ ____ ____ ____

____ ___ _____.

14. *Will Rogers (part Cherokee)*

A	T	T	E		
BUT	COME	DIDN'T	FOREFATHERS		
O		**M**	**E**	**H**	**B**	**T**
MAYFLOWER		MY	ON	OVER	THE	THEY

____ ____ ____ ____ ____ ____ ____ ____,

____ ____ ___ ___ ____.

15. *Hermione Gingold*

H	N	O	T	W
BELIEF	CONTRARY	DO	ENGLISH	NOT
G	**I**	**S**	**N**	**G**
POPULAR	TO	TWEED	WEAR	WOMEN

____ ____ ____ ____, ____ ____ ____ ____

____ ____ _____.

16. *John F. Kennedy*

L	I	N	S	A	S
EVEN	FAST	HAS	MOVE	STATES	THE
L	**D**	**T**		**T**	
TO	TO	UNITED		VERY	

____ ____ ____ ____ ____ ____ ____ ____

____ ____ _____ _____.

17. *Lawrence J. Peter*

O	*G*	*T*	*I*		*T*
AGE	IS	IT	LONGER		MIDDLE
E	*T*	*D*	*R*	*E*	
REST	TAKES	THAN	TO	WHEN	

____ ____ ____ ____ ____ ____ ____ ____

____ ____ __ ___ _____.

18. *Robert Graves*

E	*R*	*E*	*N*	*H*	*O*
BUT	IN	IN	MONEY	NO	NO
E	*Y*	*I*	*M*	*T*	
POETRY	POETRY	THEN	THERE'S	THERE'S	

____ ____ ____ ____ ____, ____ ____ ____

____ ____ ____ _____ _____.

19. *Gore Vidal*

K	*N*	*E*	*T*	*O*	*J*
AND	COULD	CULTURE	HAVE	HEMINGWAY	LIKE
E	*E*	*H*		*E*	*S*
NOT	OTHER	PRODUCED		SOMEONE	WHAT

____ ____ ____ ____ ____ ____ ____ ____

____ ____ ____ ____ ___ ____?

20. *André Maurois*

N	E	A	E	Z
ALONE	BECOME	BEING	CONSIDER	MAY

C	I	R	A	I	M	D
NEVER	TO	USED	WHEN	YOU	YOU	YOURSELF

____ ____ ____ ____ ____ ____ ____ ____,

____ ____ ____ ____ _ _ _ _ _ _ _ _ _ _ _.

21. *Ralph Waldo Emerson*

T	T	A	H	I	E
AGAINST	AND	AUTHOR'S	BOOK	FAME	HAS

L	G	E	T	P	E
LEARNING	NAME	ON	THE	THE	WRITTEN

____ ____ ____ ____ ____ ____ ____ ____

____ ____ ____ ____ _ _ _ _ _ _ _ _ _ _ _.

22. *Peter DeVries*

H	S	Y	T	U	E
ARE	BUT	FEEDING	LIKE	MOUTH	NOTHING

B	I	O	T	A	T
PARENTHOOD	SEEMS	THE	THERE	TIMES	WHEN

____ ____ ____ ____ ____ ____ ____ ____

____ ____ ____ ____ _ _ _ _ _ _ _ _ _ _ _.

23. *Dick Gregory*

O	E		N	H		T	R	E
A	ABOUT		BIT	HAPPEN		I	KNOW	QUITE

I		G		N	E		H	T
SOUTH		SPENT		THE	TO		TWENTY	YEARS

____ ____ ____ ____ ____ ____ ____

____ ____. ____ ____ ____ _____ ___

_____.

24. *Henry David Thoreau*

T	N	N		I		A
A	ARE	CONCEAL		GREAT		IF

O			D		E	
IMPROVEMENT			INVENTED		NEWSPAPERS	

N	V		I	A		B
ON	THOUGHT		TO	WERE		WORDS

____ ____ ____ ____ ____ ____ ____, ____

____ ____ ____ ____ ____ _ ___

_____.

GRID

PUZZLES

INSTRUCTIONS

Missing Links (pages 124–131)

Each grid shows an incomplete crisscross grid. Fill in the 15 letters below the grid to obtain an interlocking set of common words reading across and down. Cross off the letters as you use them, since each is used only once. Answers start on page 253.

Boomerangs (pages 132–147)

Every answer is a six-letter word that reads down, starting and ending at the number corresponding to the clue. Words read clockwise and counterclockwise as indicated. Answers on pages 257–260.

Cross Anagrams (pages 148–163)

Every answer is a six-letter word that reads left to right in the row that corresponds to the clue number. One letter of each word is given. In each puzzle grid, words in identically numbered rows are anagrams, so getting one word will help you figure out the same row in the other grid. Answers start on page 261.

Word Spiral (pages 164–179)

Words are to be entered either counterclockwise (inward) or clockwise (outward) in the indicated spaces. Every space will be used twice—once in an inward word and once in an outward word. Answers on pages 263–266.

Cross-O (pages 180–187)

Hidden in the squares are four (or, in the six-by-six puzzles, five) items in a specific category as well as the category itself. Words are found by taking the letters from one box in each of the columns in order, from left to right. Each box will be used only once, so you can cross off a box once you've used it. Answers on page 267.

Weaving (pages 188–195)

Answers to Weavers clues form a continuous chain, with the first letter in the starred space, the next four letters in the numbered spaces, the next letter in the semicircular space adjoining space four, and so on, shuttling back and forth across and around the diagram. Answer to Ring clues run sequentially in the corresponding ring; the numbered space will contain one of the letters from the answer to Clue a (not necessarily the first letter). Answers on pages 268–271.

Quadrants (pages 196–203)

The diagram's bars roughly divide it into four sections, each to accommodate eight six-letter answers, four across and four down. In addition, there are another eight six-letter answers to be entered in the center section of the diagram. Within each of these five sections, the clues are listed randomly. Answers start on page 272.

Catching Some Z's (pages 204–211)

Answers to each set of clues 1–8 run sequentially, starting in the northwesternmost numbered triangle, then going right, then down left, then right again, following the path to connect the same-numbered triangles to form a Z pattern. Answers start on page 276.

Target Practice (pages 212–217)

Each six-letter answer is to be entered, one letter per ring, starting in the numbered space and reading inward (clockwise or counterclockwise, as indicated) in adjoining spaces. Answers start on page 280.

Round the Bend (pages 218–223)

Answers to Across and Down clues (each five letters long) are to be entered normally. Answers to Bent clues begin in the numbered square and read counterclockwise, finishing at the puzzle's border (except for 12-Bent, which reads clockwise in a full circle). Answers start on page 283.

Helter-Skelter (pages 224–229)

Each answer begins in the correspondingly numbered square and reads in a straight line, finishing at or beyond the square with the next higher number. Answers on pages 285–286.

MISSING LINKS 1

	R	I	B	S		B	E	T
A			O					U
R		P	A	L				S
	P	E	R					S
U		A	D		E			L
S					A	P	S	E
E		L	A	I	R		H	
S	O						E	
	N		A	G	E	N	D	A

A	A	A	C	C

D	E	I	L	N

O	R	R	T	Y

MISSING LINKS 2

			T	H	E			
A	N				D		A	M
G					G		I	
E	X	T	E	R	I	O	R	S
N		A			N		Y	
T	A	X	I		E			
	M	E			S			
S	I	S			S	I	N	G
	D					F		O

A	A	A	A	D

D	M	M	N	N

R	S	U	Y	Y

MISSING LINKS 3

		R	E	S	I	D	E
A	N					E	
I		R	A	R	E		
R					P		
W		F					
A		L	I	N	E		
Y	A	H	O	O			
S		E	N	D	S		

A	A	C	D	F

F	F	G	I	I

L	L	N	N	S

MISSING LINKS 4

	V	E	R	S	E		S
P		G		A		P	I
A		O	P	T	I	O	N
L	E	T				S	
S		I				T	
		S					
O		T	O	Y			
H	A	S					

A	D	E	F	I
I	L	L	O	O
O	P	S	T	Y

MISSING LINKS 5

				R	A	C	Y
D		O			D	O	E
A	P	R	I	C	O	T	
M	A					E	X
		O				R	
	A	R	C			I	
		A		M		E	
	E	L	D	E	R	S	

A	A	A	C	C

C	H	I	N	O

P	R	T	T	U

MISSING LINKS 6

	O		O	R	B		
	D	O			E		C
	O				L		O
	M	I	S	S	I	O	N
	E		I		E		E
	T		R	A	V	E	S
R	E	C	E	D	E		
	R				R		

A	C	E	M	N

N	O	P	R	S

T	U	V	Y	Y

MISSING LINKS 7

	A	C	H	E			
	D		E			Y	E
			R	A	G	E	
R			O		A	S	P
A		H	I		T		O
M	E	A	N		E		S
		L			S		S
	N	O	S				E

A	A	C	D	E

E	E	E	M	O

O	R	T	U	Y

MISSING LINKS 8

		T	H	R	O	B	
	S	H	E			A	
		A	R	M		R	
P	A	N				K	
L		E		T			
U	P			O			
M	E			W	E	P	T
	G	R	I	N			O

A	A	B	D	E

E	E	E	E	E

K	K	M	S	Y

BOOMERANGS 1

CLOCKWISE
1 Matched up, as socks
2 T-shirt size
3 Droopy-eared dog
4 Embankments
5 One who destroys public property
6 Action, to a war veteran
7 Knockout of a drink
8 Atlanta Braves owner Ted
9 Tchaikovsky offering

COUNTERCLOCKWISE
2 Riotous confusion
3 Lebanon's capital
4 Women of refinement
5 Large ship
6 Warning
7 Weekend follower
8 Lumberjack's cry
9 Pail
10 January's birthstone

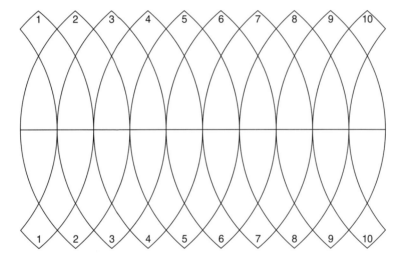

BOOMERANGS 2

CLOCKWISE

1 Cardboard box
2 Bizet heroine
3 Declare null and void
4 *Cabaret* setting
5 Nursery color, often
6 Two-wheeled carriage
7 Football player who is used on fourth and long
8 Begin a voyage
9 Kind of truck

COUNTERCLOCKWISE

2 Steep-sided valley
3 Price-regulating international syndicate
4 Mixologists
5 SAT taker's need
6 Noted neighborhood in Manhattan
7 Priest in charge of a church
8 Trite end of a movie western
9 Like repressed feelings
10 Refrain from participating in

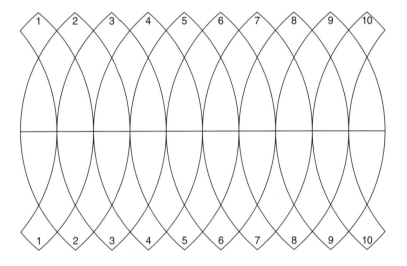

BOOMERANGS 3

CLOCKWISE
1 Montana's capital
2 Hermits
3 Small café
4 In a feeble manner
5 Very small
6 Wall Street worker
7 Part of a train
8 Arrange
9 Apartment dweller

COUNTERCLOCKWISE
2 Lousy cars
3 Ravel masterpiece
4 Port producer
5 Mortar's companion
6 Chemist's glassware
7 Milwaukee baseball player
8 Examine
9 Politician's promise
10 Above and ___ the call of duty

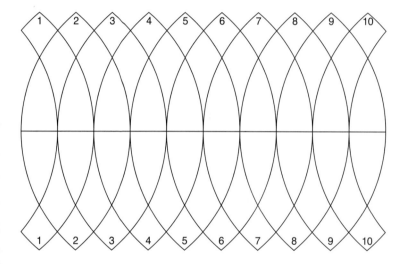

BOOMERANGS 4

CLOCKWISE
1 Dry measure equal to four pecks
2 Wooden hammer
3 Time by which a child must be home
4 Somewhat
5 Kind of harm
6 Insurance document
7 "Scat!"
8 Front of a building
9 Green film

COUNTERCLOCKWISE
2 Colonial firearm
3 Popular nut
4 One of the simple machines
5 Pub regular
6 Corpulent
7 Women's cross-laced outer garment
8 Catlike
9 Structure with curving roofs
10 Empty, as a lot

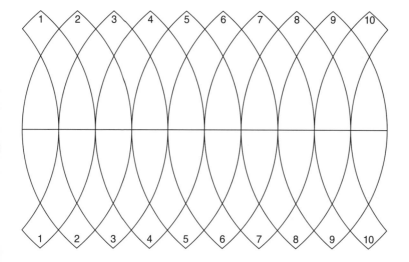

BOOMERANGS 5

CLOCKWISE

  1 Inscription site, perhaps
  2 Low-cost lodging
  3 Throat
  4 Wise counselor
  5 Low-lying grassland
  6 Harsh and loud
  7 Searches blindly
  8 Wanted badly
  9 Kind of scream

COUNTERCLOCKWISE

  2 Fairy tale boy
  3 Stemmed drinking vessel
  4 Pass ___ (be adequate)
  5 Well-aged, as wine
  6 Determined
  7 Report card listing
  8 Drove loco
  9 Move forward
 10 Necktie

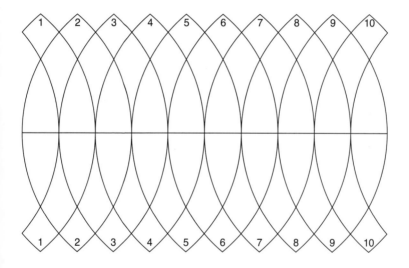

BOOMERANGS 6

CLOCKWISE
1 Theft
2 Dressing table
3 Chess player's move
4 Transcendental meditation user's utterance
5 Famed orator
6 "Geronimo!," e.g.
7 Kitchen appliances
8 Overseas correspondent
9 Lament

COUNTERCLOCKWISE
2 Drag through the mud
3 *In Cold Blood* author
4 Envelope type
5 Havana honcho
6 Cold and snowy
7 Indy cars
8 FedEx delivery
9 Tiger type
10 Spare seeker's target, often

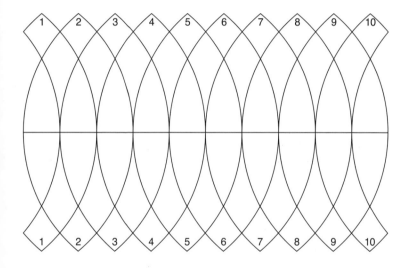

BOOMERANGS 7

CLOCKWISE

1 Dumpling in Chinese soup
2 Pitcher
3 Sausage, to a Brit
4 By a narrow margin
5 Parris Island figure
6 Inventor's quest
7 Losing color
8 Mourn aloud
9 Servile follower

COUNTERCLOCKWISE

2 Scary movie genre
3 Pitcher at the plate, often
4 Brewer's ingredient
5 Mess up through ineptitude
6 Dad or mom
7 Getting along
8 Present but not visible
9 Cargo
10 Walk-on parts

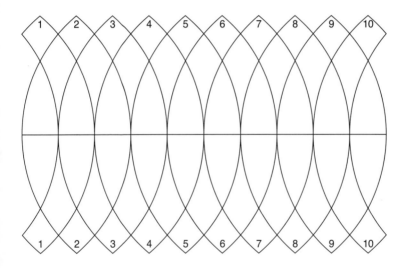

BOOMERANGS 8

CLOCKWISE
1 Region between hills
2 Church doctrines
3 More zany
4 Greek or Macedonian
5 Grifter
6 Sign before Aries
7 Hire
8 Do a cartographer's job
9 Excite

COUNTERCLOCKWISE
2 An O is made up of three of these in Morse code
3 Buck
4 Payoff money collectors
5 Ankle-length garment
6 Accordion numbers
7 1987 Danny DeVito comedy
8 Yale's bulldog, e.g.
9 Kind of call
10 Shirk a responsibility

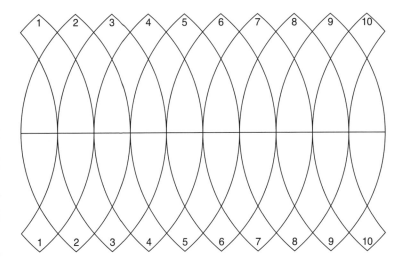

CROSS ANAGRAMS 1

1 D					
2	I				
3		E			
4			S		
5				E	
6					L

1 Sock mender
2 The art of motion pictures
3 Gathers bit by bit
4 Velvet Elvis paintings and similar art
5 More chic
6 Give an in-depth account

1	E					
2		N				
3			G			
4				I		
5					N	
6						E

1 Trip to the dry cleaner, for example
2 Lacking red blood cells
3 Pinhead dancers?
4 Show biz routine
5 Figure out the bearings of
6 Widen, as pupils

CROSS ANAGRAMS 2

	1	2	3	4	5	6
1	E					
2		A				
3			S			
4				T		
5					E	
6						R

1 Pass, as time
2 The ___ State (Wisconsin)
3 Spoke in a grating tone
4 More rapid
5 Shook off, as pursuers
6 Glowing object that is falling from space

P					
	A				
		R			
			A		
				D	
					E

1 Word in a polite request
2 ___ in on (rudely interfered)
3 Apply butter to bread
4 Attack from a plane with a machine gun
5 Deceive
6 Television channel changer

CROSS ANAGRAMS 3

R					
	E				
		C			
			O		
				R	
					D

1 Most ready to eat
2 Pandemonium
3 Scarflike neckties
4 Decked in the boxing ring
5 Cling (to)
6 Word on a wanted poster

1 P					
2	L				
3		A			
4			Y		
5				E	
6					R

1 Man of the cloth
2 Found fault with
3 Seashores
4 Green-lighted
5 Soccer player's move
6 Sock storage site

CROSS ANAGRAMS 4

	C				
1	C				
2		A			
3			R		
4				B	
5					O
6					

(Grid with C in row 1 col 1, A in row 2 col 2, R in row 3 col 3, B in row 4 col 4, O in row 5 col 5, N in row 6 col 6)

1 Paddled down a river
2 Small taste of food
3 Highlander's design
4 Expel from the legal profession
5 Protestant minister
6 Space around the edge of a printed page

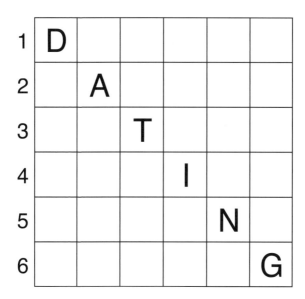

1 Member of the clergy
2 Syrup-producing trees
3 Wickerwork material
4 Pigtails, e.g.
5 Cooks' protective garments
6 Preparing for battle

CROSS ANAGRAMS 5

1 P					
2	E				
3		A			
4			N		
5				U	
6					T

1 Naval academy freshmen
2 Professor's goal
3 Radio interference
4 They're heard at protest rallies
5 Off-color, as a joke
6 Clandestine

B					
	U				
		T			
			T		
				E	
					R

1 Censor's sounds
2 Soup server
3 Top floors of houses
4 Clean and jerk's counterpart
5 24-sheet paper sets
6 Quantity with magnitude and direction

CROSS ANAGRAMS 6

	1	2	3	4	5	6
1	F					
2		I				
3			G			
4				U		
5					R	
6						E

1 Robin Hood's home
2 Face, slangily
3 Think highly of
4 Gumshoe
5 Part of speech that often ends with "ly"
6 Group of thespians

1 S					
2	K				
3		A			
4			T		
5				E	
6					R

1 More like a baby's bottom
2 Mogul hoppers
3 Teacher, at times
4 Charlie ___ (Pete Rose's nickname)
5 Confronted with courage
6 Sullen person

CROSS ANAGRAMS 7

1 B					
2	O				
3		T			
4			T		
5				L	
6					E

1 Supervisors
2 Subjects of conversation
3 One who soaks in a tub
4 Engine component
5 Military decorations
6 Semiconscious state

1 O					
2	P				
3		E			
4			N		
5				E	
6					R

1 Excessively preoccupy the mind of
2 Physics subject dealing with light
3 Exhalation
4 Scoreboard units
5 Maiden who may be "in distress"
6 Peach drink

CROSS ANAGRAMS 8

1 T					
2	U				
3		N			
4			N		
5				E	
6					L

1 Collections of treasures
2 Bucolic
3 Slightly charred
4 Black eye
5 Went berserk
6 Christmas tree embellishment

	V					
1	V					
2		I				
3			S			
4				I		
5					O	
6						N

1 Ballot casters
2 Like an orange
3 Plan out in the mind
4 Hallowed place
5 Magazine employee
6 Pay attention

WORD SPIRAL 1

INWARD

1-6	Homicide
7-12	Rifle loader of yore
13-21	Occurring when the sun is down
22-27	Hyundai house
28-33	Decorative tile picture
34-43	Window washer's precautionary accessory
44-50	Having left a valid will

OUTWARD

50-47	State: Fr.
46-41	Reach an agreement out of court
40-37	Computer data-storage unit
36-30	Flat pieces used as molding
29-25	End of an alphabet
24-19	Loose overcoat
18-16	Monotonous routine
15-10	Bird with a wide wingspan
9-4	Damaged
3-1	Cuba libre ingredient

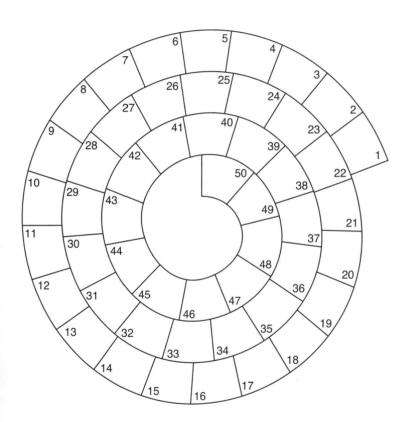

WORD SPIRAL 2

INWARD

1-4	Moistens
5-10	Weak
11-21	County fair event
22-26	Chasm
27-33	Neighbor of Morocco and Tunisia
34-37	Russian ruler
38-44	Cost of a flight
45-50	Diacritical mark that indicates a long vowel

OUTWARD

50-48	"Conjunction Junction" word
47-42	Photojournalist's tool
41-37	Cloister denizen
36-30	*Top Hat* dancer
29-24	Like tired eyes
23-18	Muddle
17-15	Balderdash, to a Brit
14-9	Price-controlling group
8-1	Diner entrée

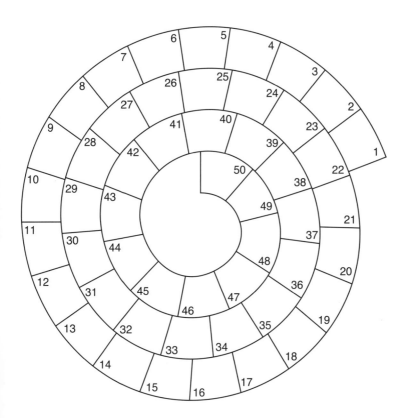

WORD SPIRAL 3

INWARD

1-5	Sting operation
6-13	Marginal text
14-18	West Point student
19-27	Donnybrook
28-31	Went United
32-42	Theatrical offering
43-45	Museum offering
46-50	Cut

OUTWARD

50-48	Morning moisture
47-42	Way off course
41-38	Sample record
37-33	Panatela, e.g.
32-26	Shakespeare's ___ *Night*
25-22	Present
21-16	Treated some flour
15-9	Flammable solvent
8-1	Heated exchanges

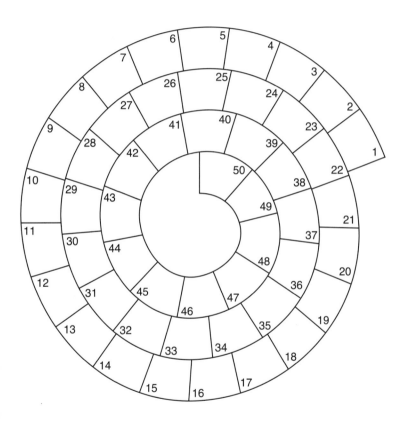

WORD SPIRAL 4

INWARD

1-6	Call it a career
7-11	"The Pine Tree State"
12-18	"Just the facts, ma'am" series
19-27	Cooking oil source
28-31	Baa maids?
32-41	"Ode to Duty" author
42-50	Highway safety feature

OUTWARD

50-47	Pinocchio, for one
46-40	Beer from a tap, to a Brit
39-36	Obeys the coxswain
35-30	Start to nod off
29-22	Lycanthrope
21-16	Make secure
15-8	Shrub with white or yellow flowers
7-1	Deserving person

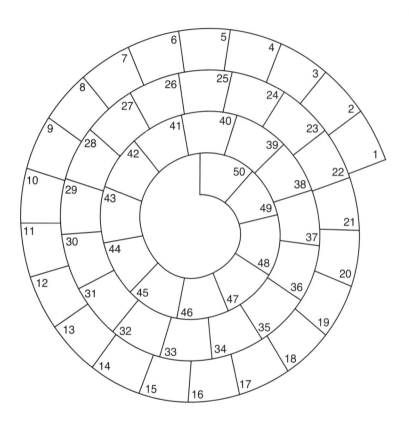

WORD SPIRAL 5

INWARD

1-5	Blackboard material
6-13	Rule out in advance
14-18	Circus worker
19-23	Hooded snake
24-28	Swamp critter: Var.
29-32	Pesky little bug
33-39	Working stiff's strenuous daily activity
40-45	Kid's noisy toy
46-50	Building material for one of the Three Little Pigs

OUTWARD

50-47	Skin protuberance
46-43	Cozy
42-36	Vehicle used at a racetrack
35-30	Highland cloth
29-20	*Ninotchka* star
19-12	Laid on a pyre
11-7	Worrier's stomach problem
6-1	"She loves me, she loves me not" items

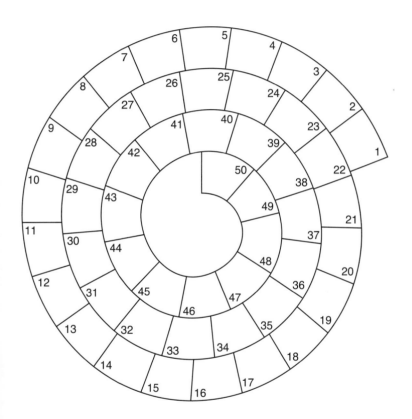

WORD SPIRAL 6

INWARD

1-8	Conference attendees' badges
9-15	Spell-casting craft
16-23	Escape hatch, perhaps
24-30	Some infielders
31-37	Former Chrysler bigwig
38-44	Aquatic rodent
45-50	Make a boo-boo

OUTWARD

50-46	Tutor's charge
45-41	Like a wasteland
40-36	Red-berried poisonous shrub
35-29	"Snow," to a drug pusher
28-25	Flatland
24-20	Dwell gloomily on a subject
19-15	Politico's group
14-8	Traverse the road twice
7-1	Sentry

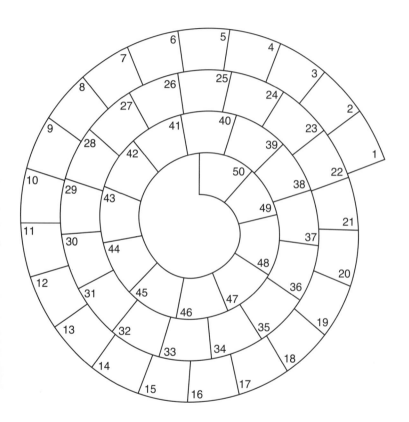

WORD SPIRAL 7

INWARD

1-5	Kind of saxophone
6-10	Beaded calculators
11-16	Created anew
17-25	Canapé spread
26-29	Place to get a latte
30-36	Commuters' computers
37-43	Wear and tear
44-47	Attention seeker's sound
48-50	Hound sound

OUTWARD

50-46	Chassis
45-41	City on the Songka River
40-33	Touchy subject
32-25	White person to a Native American, in old movies
24-22	Noisy dance genre
21-15	Detested
14-8	It was named after Vespucci
7-1	Rank of honor above a knight

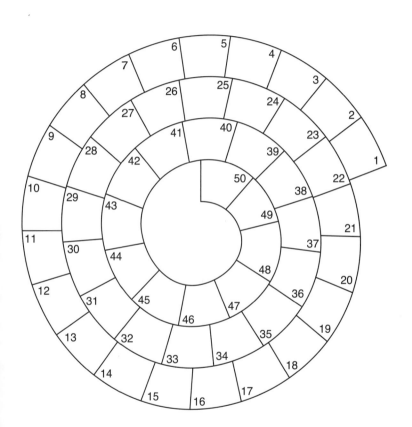

WORD SPIRAL 8

INWARD

1-5	Nora Ephron's screenwriter sister
6-13	Old maid
14-21	Apache leader whose name is shouted by skydivers
22-27	Dab
28-36	Completely overwhelmed
37-39	Noisy commotion
40-46	Ousted Panamanian leader
47-50	Boastfully assert

OUTWARD

50-44	Trash
43-36	Garden gate feature
35-32	Brusque
31-29	Use a Singer
28-23	Moon mission name
22-17	Dotted tile
16-11	Lament
10-7	Small cut
6-1	Went boating

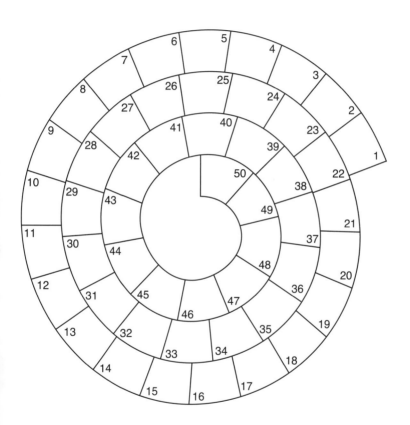

CROSS-O 1

M	U	L	CH	E	D
K	E	D	A	S	R
O	N	P	I	ME	P
C	E	T	I	N	H
P	ON	I	P	R	S
R	E	ST	O	U	NT

Category: _____

_____   _____

_____   _____

_____

CROSS-O 2

BA	L	DW	IN	E
PI	S	U	O	ET
C	L	S	T	O
W	C	AR	I	ON
F	OO	C	OL	ND

Category: _____

_____   _____

_____   _____

CROSS-O 3

S	U	N	T	E	L
C	P	E	U	N	R
G	R	AN	I	E	R
F	R	AT	NS	L	ER
ST	T	A	N	E	L
U	OL	A	D	I	A

Category: _____

_____   _____

_____   _____

_____

CROSS-O 4

C	L	O	N	E	R
LI	F	P	EN	I	L
AD	E	I	I	A	AL
CO	M	UT	E	CE	L
G	A	N	TA	A	NT
O	E	F	R	R	N

Category: _____

_____   _____

_____   _____

_____

CROSS-O 5

C	A	N	O	N
R	I	T	E	D
L	W	B	RI	N
T	O	Y	E	C
F	A	E	T	ON

Category: _____

_____   _____

_____   _____

CROSS-O 6

N	O	M	A	N	S
C	AR	L	R	AN	A
B	S	ZE	A	C	D
I	Y	R	SI	DO	D
C	U	B	AL	U	RA
S	EW	P	A	T	S

Category: _____

_____   _____

_____   _____

_____

CROSS-O 7

H	A	CK	B	O	Y
L	AB	R	S	A	RD
CA	U	N	O	G	T
B	A	RI	D	OA	M
S	U	N	IA	LE	U
C	R	R	R	E	E

Category: _____

_____   _____

_____   _____

_____

CROSS-O 8

P	RA	N	S	E
A	I	R	MI	AN
M	AL	T	I	NG
H	US	B	A	NO
P	O	O	T	O

Category: _____

_____   _____

_____   _____

WEAVING 1

WEAVERS

a   Actor whose uncle is Francis Ford Coppola: 2 wds.

b   Shake in the grass?

c   A silk hat brought him to life

d   He had a Top-10 hit with 1994's "Loser"

e   Much loafing is done there

f   Most silly

g   Pearl Mosque locale

h   Wherewithal

i   Bet both ways

j   Sign painter's skill

k   Montaigne output

l   Turns the ignition key: 2 wds.

m   Navy mascot

n   *To Kill a Mockingbird*'s Radley

o   Goolagong of tennis

p   All ___ (clumsy)

q   Tall, slender champagne glasses

RING 1

a   Item on a tourist's itinerary

b   Large body of troops

c   Orderly

d   Austrian opera conductor Karl

RING 2

a   Inasmuch as

b   Worker who uses glossy paint

c   Correct a correction

RING 3

a   Time piece?

b   Had brunch

c   Indication of a possessive woman?

d   Most debonair

RING 4

a   Cough syrup dosages, often

b   Where to find the USA's only diamond mine

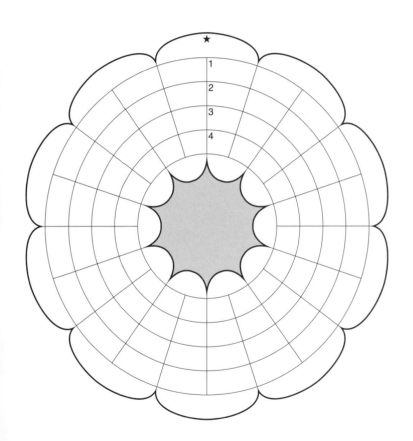

WEAVING 2

WEAVERS

a Resort island near
   Nantucket: 2 wds.
b Paper used for legal pads
c Standards
d Massachusetts city where
   volleyball was invented
e 1952 Eddie Fisher song:
   2 wds.
f Contour
g Gentlewoman
h Pompous
i Pastoral Kenyan tribe
j Unbroken
k Shuffleboard stick
l Crossword diagram
m Signaled, as on *Win Ben
   Stein's Money*: 2 wds.
n Half a Steinbeck title:
   2 wds.
o Home of Henry VIII's first
   wife
p 1954 mutant-ant movie

RING 1

a Red, white, green :
   Hungary :: black, red, gold :
   ___
b Paulo preceder
c Triangular street sign
d Capital of Bangladesh: Var.

RING 2

a Shot from above?: 2 wds.
b Seeing things?
c Goldfinger's first name

RING 3

a Rembrandt's ___ *Watch*
b Count loved by Anna
   Karenina
c Tacit

RING 4

a Fluttering insects named
   for a woman in Greek
   myth: 2 wds.
b Judge who framed Roger
   Rabbit
c Designating

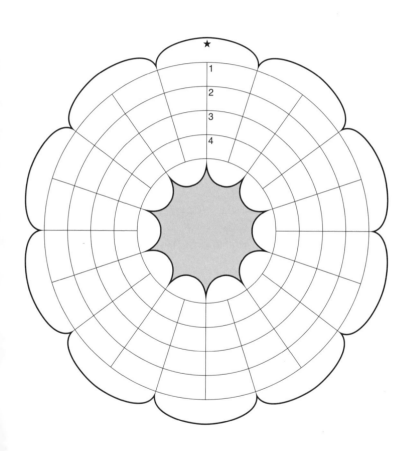

WEAVING 3

WEAVERS

a   *Odd Couple*'s neat half:
    2 wds.
b   House Minority Leader
    from 1994–2002 (D-MO)
c   Emblem of Erato or
    Terpsichore
d   Breed of steed with speed
e   Indispensable
f   Hotel employee
g   Refer (to)
h   Bulletin board accessories
i   Letter resembling a capital
    O with a superimposed
    hyphen
j   Tropical monkey or embar-
    rassing gaffe
k   Piece of snooker equip-
    ment: 2 wds.
l   Statement of religious
    belief
m   Round of gunfire
n   Young women, to
    Crocodile Dundee
o   Arena supplanted by the
    Georgia Dome
p   Mothers of Invention
    leader
q   *Odd Couple*'s sloppy half:
    2 wds.

RING 1

a   Less bananas?
b   Pinkerton Agency logo
c   Gymnast Gaylord
d   French-speaking Belgian

RING 2

a   Do improv, psychothera-
    peutically: Hyph.
b   Site of Northern Illinois
    University: 2 wds.
c   Othello's lieutenant

RING 3

a   Deliver the lines cold:
    Hyph.
b   Take the wheel
c   Outcry that turned Billy
    Batson into Captain
    Marvel

RING 4

a   Paris street known for its
    retail stores: 4 wds.
b   Zilch
c   Title tec in a 1971 Donald
    Sutherland movie

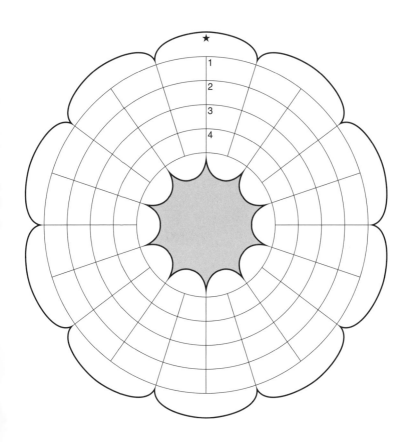

WEAVING 4

WEAVERS

a Pole staff?
b St. ___ (two-time
   Olympics site)
c Mencken and Hunt: Abbr.
d Cry from a surprised Brit
e Western horse
f Palindromic preposition
g Had the desired effect
h Soon-to-be non-bachelor
i *Rebel Without a Cause*
   actor
j Wintered with the birds:
   2 wds.
k Dressy apparel: 2 wds.
l French article
m Clearasil target
n 100 decades
o Command to Rover
p Block and tackle, e.g.
q Mint condition
r Summertime quaff:
   2 wds., var.

RING 1

a Rich
b Scintilla
c Verdict in *12 Angry Men*:
   2 wds.

RING 2

a Power to cause bad luck:
   2 wds.
b Bob who played Captain
   Kangaroo for over 30 years
c Interlocks

RING 3

a Fenway Park's left-field
   fence: 2 wds.
b He's looking rather blue
c Fit of hysteria, to Bart
   Simpson

RING 4

a Periodic payments for life
b Kimono accessory
c Long-popular "Must-See
   TV" entry

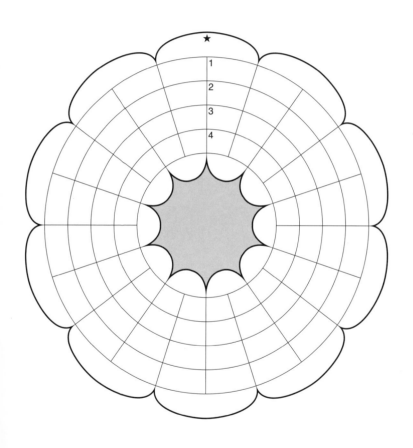

QUADRANTS 1

NORTHWEST
a About 3.5 million square miles, mostly sand
b Athabaskan language
c Bearse of *Married ... With Children*
d Fast-growing softwood tree
e Hardly dense
f Moore's hubby in *Ghost*
g Singer/actress Pia
h Stocky, burrowing marsupial

NORTHEAST
a Bad news for the manufacturer
b Finally: 2 wds.
c Gracefully slender
d Main thoroughfare
e Nauseatingly coy
f Passes along
g Petty organization?
h Red Bordeaux

SOUTHWEST
a Baby
b Edberg of tennis
c Enter hostile territory
d Feel a strong need (for)

e Philippines' "Iron Butterfly"
f Punctual: 2 wds.
g Use Scope
h Welsh dogs

SOUTHEAST
a *Cabaret* venue, the ___ Klub: 2 wds.
b Crooner Julius: 2 wds.
c Like T-shirts and jeans, e.g.
d Nocturnal lizards
e Octogenarian's next milestone
f One of Lucille's costars
g Opposite of "Attention!": 2 wds.
h Sentence structure

CENTER
a *Beach Blanket Bingo* outfit
b Book following Acts
c Calm
d Drawing pen
e Liable to erupt
f Shul staff
g Swap commodities
h Try hard

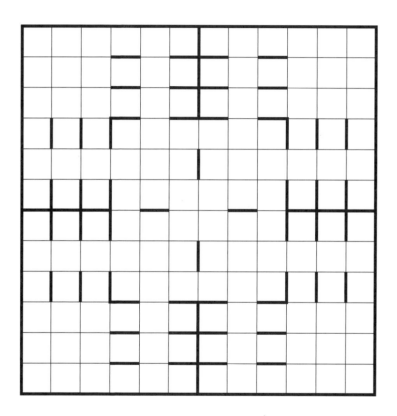

QUADRANTS 2

NORTHWEST
a Eggs: Spanish
b Grave
c June 6–7 endurance race site: 2 wds.
d Marathon runner Joan
e Maximally: 2 wds.
f Picture made of inlaid bits
g Run-down
h Vent

NORTHEAST
a Angora
b Blow reveille
c Croupier's task
d Frisbee prototype: 2 wds.
e Jim Varney character
f 1912 Olympian in a Burt Lancaster biopic
g One of Gilligan's co-islanders
h Singer Morissette

SOUTHWEST
a Electronics nut
b ___ K. Le Guin (sci-fi writer)
c 1975 James Clavell novel
d MacArthur said he would

e *My Favorite Year* star
f Playground piece
g Spectrum producers
h "That's putting it ___"

SOUTHEAST
a Declare positively
b *Growing Pains* star
c Hercules's companion
d Hit the road
e Leader of the Grateful Dead
f "Nearer, My God, ___": 2 wds.
g Religious Friend
h Vocation

CENTER
a Charlie Brown's creator
b Dag Hammarskjöld's successor: 2 wds.
c Dan who played the father in *The Wonder Years*
d Executor's responsibility
e Handled roughly
f Imam's place
g Shine brilliantly
h Silicon dioxide

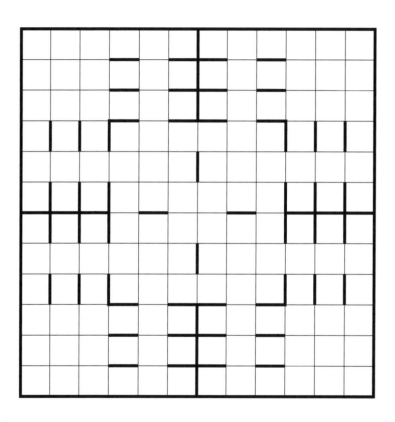

QUADRANTS 3

NORTHWEST
a Antonio's defender
b Golden-skinned, juicy fruit
c Green-lit
d ___-mâché
e Most mature
f Spain plus Portugal
g "___, That's My Baby":
   2 wds.
h With hands on hips

NORTHEAST
a Corresponds
b Cowboy's ropes
c Debate participant
d Ice cream parlor supply
e Like most Manhattan
   streets: Hyph.
f Nashville-based TV series,
   1969–1992: 2 wds.
g Nova Scotia cape
h Went in search of

SOUTHWEST
a Cease
b Dumb
c Flyer out of Townsville,
   perhaps
d Harmful intent

e Highlander's plaid
f Occupation in an O'Neill
   title
g Party animal?
h Sunsweet product

SOUTHEAST
a Alternative to alpine
b Bluesy Cajun dance music
c Cultural agcy. of the United
   Nations
d German
e Just about
f Medical center
g Mountebanks
h Produce harmony

CENTER
a Follower of Lao-tzu
b Ingratiate
c In the neighborhood
d Long way to get there
e Monticello or Mount
   Vernon
f Off the blackboard
g Philippine ex-president
   Corazon
h Sunni's counterpart

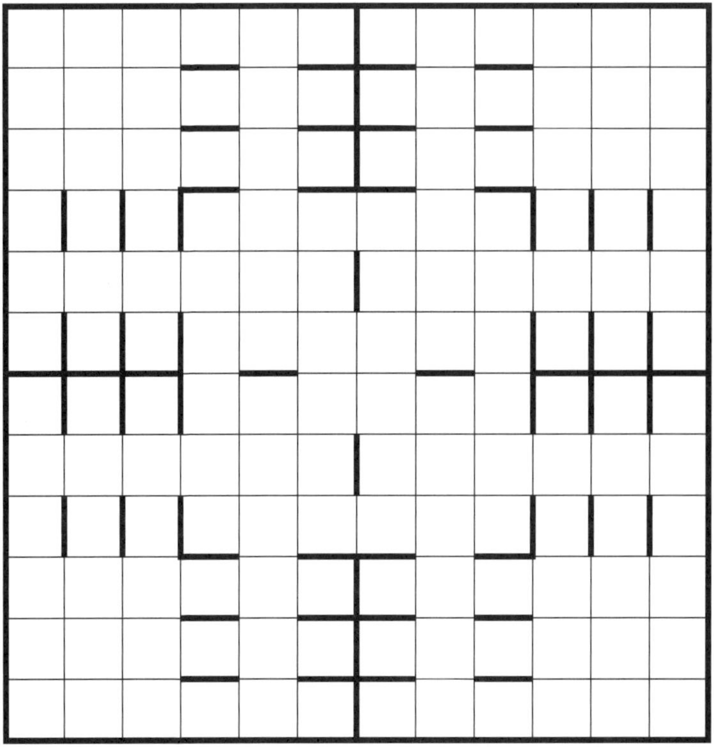

QUADRANTS 4

NORTHWEST
a Apply a T-shirt decal: 2 wds.
b California surfers' haven
c Ferdinand's kingdom
d Hogan occupants
e Love apple
f Measure of ft^3 or dB
g Williams of *Poltergeist*
h WWII Pacific Fleet commander

NORTHEAST
a Cassius : Muhammad :: Lew : ___
b Duration
c He carries out orders
d Indulges in libel
e Leaves in the fridge overnight
f Stowe's cruel taskmaster
g Supreme Court justice, 1955–1971
h Surrey decoration

SOUTHWEST
a Big ___ (large WWI cannon)
b Goldfinger's hat-hurling aide

c "Handwriting on the wall" decipherer
d Hidden assailant
e Hot dog topping
f In abundance
g Missouri city named in "Route 66"
h Ransom note closing, maybe: 2 wds.

SOUTHEAST
a Batman's bailiwick
b Beat
c Brand of Mexican beer
d Country song?
e Unctuously servile
f White of *Family Matters*
g With cordiality
h Wizard-in-training Harry of kiddie lit

CENTER
a Exciting experience
b Fictional sleuth Queen
c Fourscore
d Late-'70s candy bar named for a ballplayer
e Nursery toy
f Pang
g Toro's offensive tactic
h Whoville killjoy

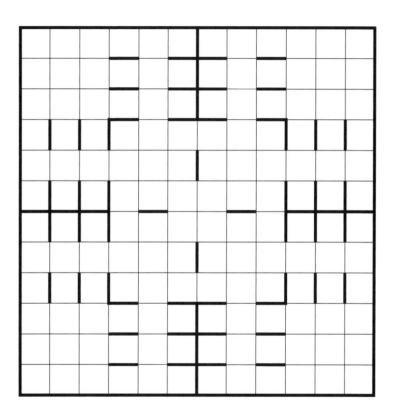

CATCHING SOME Z'S 1

CLUES

1 a Aroma, to a viniculturist
  b Port city on Honshu
  c The role of Don Giovanni is generally sung by one
  d Use an S.O.S pad
  e Stimpy's pal
  f Sisters
2 a Fire a water pistol
  b Expunge
  c Bleakly pessimistic
  d "I await your reply, good buddy"
  e Danced with a glide
3 a Swiss state
  b Singer Young
  c Leisurely stroll
  d At ease
  e Navy clerk
4 a Mediocre novel written for the money
  b Abominable Snowman
  c One of the As in "AAA": Abbr.
  d Assess
  e Director Bergman
5 a Without difficulty
  b *Jurassic Park* beast: 2 wds.
  c Knave of Hearts' booty
  d Boca ___, FL

6 a Go on a brief break: 2 wds.
  b Anyone's game?
  c Pertinacious: Hyph.
  d Former colt
7 a Brunhoff's pachyderm
  b Tryst
  c Grassy plain
  d Do some cultivating
  e Knot on a tree trunk
  f Inferior
8 a Watergate Plumbers' equipment
  b Debonair
  c Park in New York City, for example
  d Admiral who devised the Pearl Harbor attack
  e Car whose old TV ads featured a liar named Joe

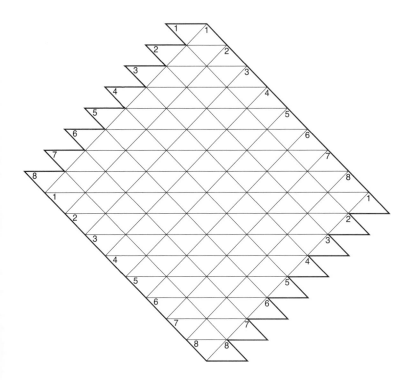

CATCHING SOME Z'S 2

CLUES

1 a Its motto is "Eureka"
  b Doesn't even get a D–
  c ___ oblige (moral duty of the wealthy)
  d Five-time World Cup finalist, three-time winner
  e Cudgel
2 a *Sexual Politics* author Kate
  b Imitation
  c Rick Blaine's portrayer
  d 1922 German film version of *Dracula*
3 a Use Snuggle
  b Treated sacrilegiously
  c Neptune or Poseidon: 2 wds.
  d Casting no vote
4 a Lacking an MPAA designation
  b Basil-based sauce
  c ___ *a Wonderful Life*
  d Scotland Yard inspector often shown up by Sherlock Holmes
  e Objet d'art
  f *An American in Paris* actress Nina
5 a Diner employees

  b Why a store may be closed for two weeks
  c Fasten your seat belt
  d Michael Keaton/Teri Garr movie: 2 wds.
6 a Stupid person
  b Tree in the pine family
  c Small circles of friends
  d Rice recipe
  e Aristophanes's forte
  f Bud's partner
  g Navigator's stack
7 a Act of bringing forth
  b Concealment
  c Kidney-shaped
  d *Saturday Night Live* alumnus
8 a Implicit
  b *Born Free* lioness
  c Adder or asp
  d Re Brunei's leader
  e Repetitive rhythm from the brass section: Hyph.

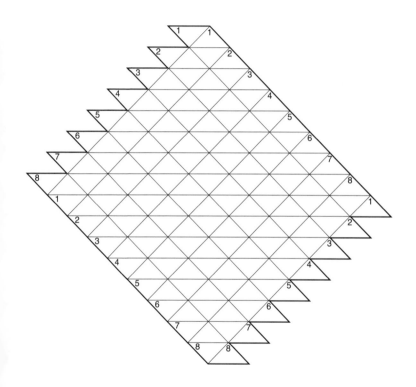

CATCHING SOME Z'S 3

CLUES

1 a Baby boomer's kid: 2 wds.
  b Re Ra
  c Northern lights: 2 wds.
  d Ready for action
  e Black-and-white diving bird
2 a Veto, in pig Latin
  b Quick snooze
  c Like some 1998–1999 class action legislation
  d *The Music Man's* Marian, et al.
3 a Hundred Years' War battle site
  b Stressed, as a syllable
  c Alimentary inflammation
  d Letter-shaped gripping devices: Hyph.
  e By inevitable predetermination
4 a Tubular, diagonally cut pasta
  b *Blanco's* opposite
  c Composer of the opera *Fiesque*
  d Citrus spread
  e One of those "three little words"
5 a Fitness expert Jack

  b Home of *Venus de Milo* and *Winged Victory*
  c Supermarket shelfful
  d Wading bird with a down-curved bill
  e Mel Tillis's footstep-following daughter
  f Dot on a map
  g Cones' retinal partners
6 a Wall at the outer edge of a rampart
  b Buddhist doctrine of deliverance
  c It's divided in two by Goat Island: 2 wds.
  d Hippolyta was one
7 a Very dry, as champagne
  b Elbow
  c Part of Eden?
  d Abu Dhabi, for example
  e What the eighth season of Dallas turned out to be
  f Christmas carol
8 a Sexy
  b Quiche ___
  c Galápagos creature
  d Comedian who hung from a clock in *Safety Last*
  e Exude slowly through a hole: 2 wds.

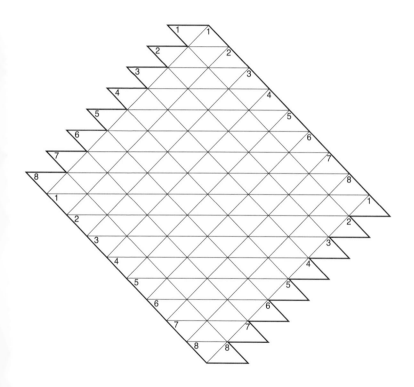

CATCHING SOME Z'S 4

CLUES

1 a Tommy Smothers is skilled with this toy
  b Queen of whodunits
  c Fashion's Armani or music's Moroder
  d Hand bone
  e Nation on a Persian Gulf peninsula
2 a Captain Janeway's starship
  b Floral emblem of the Mikado
  c Morose
  d *Plan 9 From Outer Space* vessel (truly!)
3 a Take it on the lam
  b Aplenty
  c *Liar, Liar* actress Tierney
  d Baseball club?
  e Compact: 2 wds.
  f Saharan caravan
4 a Nylon tape fastener
  b Capital of Tibet
  c Defeat soundly; or, an old 78 rpm record
  d A little night music?
  e Male chauvinist's assessment of women: 2 wds.

5 a Bitter resin, an ingredient in perfumes (Makes a great gift!)
  b Poor substitute
  c Jack Ruby's defense attorney
  d Ecclesiastic's office
  e Sam Malone, e.g.
6 a Fruits used in Newtons
  b Sweet potatoes' look-alikes
  c She threw her hat into the ring
  d Has a bug
  e Seamen's org.
  f Scrimshaw or decoupage
  g Squashed square
7 a Monetary unit of Sweden
  b *Lost in Yonkers* star
  c Youngster in an aerie
  d Birthstone for October (ancient) or March (modern)
  e Muslim temple
8 a Popular variety of pocket billiards
  b Unknowledgeable in a given field
  c Idle companion?
  d Iowa city on the Mississippi

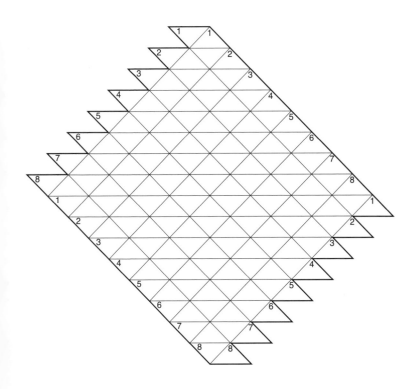

TARGET PRACTICE 1

CLOCKWISE
1 Individual
2 Erstwhile grape
3 Water slides
4 Has confidence in
5 Irascibility
6 More acidic
7 Starbucks orders
8 She played Princess Leia
9 Rent payer
10 Bump up and down roughly
11 24ths of pure gold
12 Shade of yellow
13 Form of high-speed skiing
14 Become a tenant: 2 wds.
15 Hard, chewy candy
16 Ransacked
17 Money holder
18 Brand of fabric softener
19 Former chairman of the Joint Chiefs of Staff
20 Wheedle

COUNTERCLOCKWISE
1 Sold temporarily
2 Turn thumbs down on
3 King or Lombard
4 1936 song, "___ Make You Whistle"
5 His work was done by Friday
6 One confined by infirmity: Hyph.
7 Untie
8 Imperfections
9 Brits' near-quarts
10 Crown clown
11 Labeled with a U
12 Freedom fighters have them
13 Pop ___ Junior League Football
14 Threaten
15 Until now: 2 wds.
16 Nomadic types
17 Befitting the Mrs.
18 Canadian island in the Arctic Ocean
19 Hay fever stimulus
20 Gulch

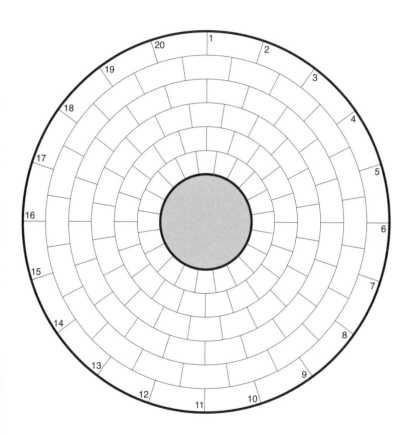

TARGET PRACTICE 2

CLOCKWISE

1 Prepared, with "up"
2 Fireman's jacket?
3 Did some woodworking
4 Incriminated fraudulently
5 Long, curling ocean wave
6 Michigan's Lower Peninsula looks like one
7 Piece of lettuce?
8 *A Doll's House* surname
9 "Peanuts" character who raises dirt wherever he goes
10 Lacks: 2 wds.
11 "Water Music" composer
12 Pleasure trip
13 Summer TV fare
14 Last bit: 2 wds.
15 Environment
16 ___ Thursday (Easter minus three)
17 Emergency prioritization
18 Speed skater Blair
19 Pleasure trips
20 Pornographic: Hyph.

COUNTERCLOCKWISE

1 Run-down and dirty
2 Skullcap
3 Nebraska river
4 Bell-bottoms
5 Deranged
6 Sounded anguished
7 Rheostat
8 Place of rapid growth
9 Threw stuff at
10 *Love Story* director, one-time AMPAS president
11 J.R. Ewing's portrayer
12 National park in Alberta
13 Hall carpet, maybe
14 One was named for Achilles
15 First little piggy's destination
16 Cervantes's first name
17 *Gong Show* display
18 Boston hockey team
19 Became a member
20 Site of Kubla Khan's pleasure dome

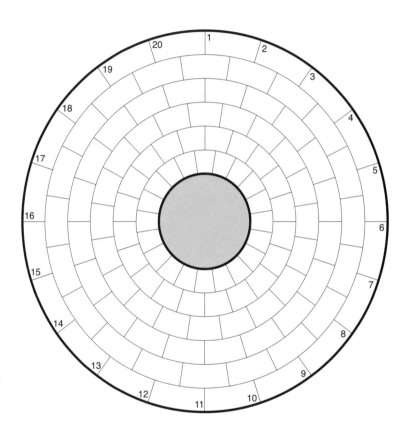

TARGET PRACTICE 3

CLOCKWISE
1 Laid-back
2 Vegetable used in Chinese food: 2 wds.
3 Entireties
4 You, now
5 Stock footage?
6 Immobilized
7 West Point freshmen
8 Dubya's first name
9 Infantry members
10 Showing distress
11 Hang around
12 Someone who puts out?
13 To speak French?
14 Appropriate
15 Financial report acronym
16 "Unromantic as ___ morning" (C. Brontë)
17 Streisand standard
18 Shadowy
19 Tommy or Jimmy of Big Band days
20 Elton's metaphor for Marilyn

COUNTERCLOCKWISE
1 Patterned like fudge ripple
2 Reflection, to Rousseau
3 One who carries a torch?
4 Half a hyphenated word meaning "show indecision"
5 Bird with a fanlike crest
6 Do surveillance on
7 Verified
8 Equipment for Lennox Lewis
9 Eccentric old coot
10 Investigations
11 Polo man
12 What's happening?
13 *Grosse ___ Blank*
14 Fries lightly
15 Tried to cure
16 *The Naked and the Dead* author
17 Bill (punny synonym for the previous answer)
18 Elvis's "Return to ___"
19 Thingamajig
20 Rival of Dell and Gateway

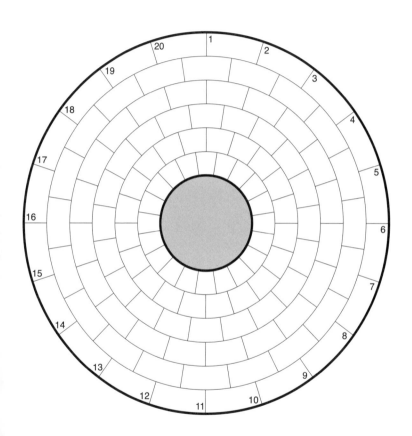

ROUND THE BEND 1

ACROSS

1 Cushioned
5 Second brightest stars
9 Astrologer Dixon
10 Put on the qui vive
14 Past or present, e.g.
15 Midway alternative
16 Honey bunch?
19 Between, in Boulogne
24 Subdued, to Stokowski
25 Soap opera extra, often
26 Poorly kept
28 Game show hosted by
   Chuck Woolery

DOWN

1 Bail out
2 Lookout point
4 Colonial lawyer Silas
5 Dueling instrument?
7 Intense devotion
8 Strunk & White's subject
16 Dance lessons
17 *Trivial Breath* poet
18 He often said, "He's dead,
   Jim"
19 Surveillance work
20 Awaken
21 Over

BENT

3 Complicate
6 Rushmore figure
11 *Aunt ___ Cope Book*
12 Late-night legend: 2 wds.
13 Key factor when starting a
   business
22 Unjustly cruel
23 Barbizon landscapist Jules
27 Ace on a par-3
29 Reddish

ROUND THE BEND 2

ACROSS
1 Grifter's ideas
5 *Maltese Falcon* tec
9 Hyundai headquarters
10 Whimpered
14 Boxer Liston
15 Lie
16 Canticle group
19 Topiarist's canvas
24 Belong: 2 wds.
25 Engage in blackmail
26 Criteria
28 Mysterious Psalms word

DOWN
1 Irving Berlin's "Blue ___"
2 Co-op's counterpart
4 Bygone mag for teen girls
5 Gushes forth
7 Exclude
8 Enlighten
16 Kirk Douglas trademark
17 *Wings on My Feet* auto-
    biographer
18 Horseman's handful
19 Competition for Capriati
20 City in New York on the
    Mohawk River
21 Pullman accommodation

BENT
3 Created a snafu: 2 wds.
6 Out of sorts?
11 Prefix for red or structure
12 Popular carol: 3 wds.
13 Pet
22 Drink that can be pink
23 Emulate
27 *Natural Born Killers*
    director
29 Described in detail

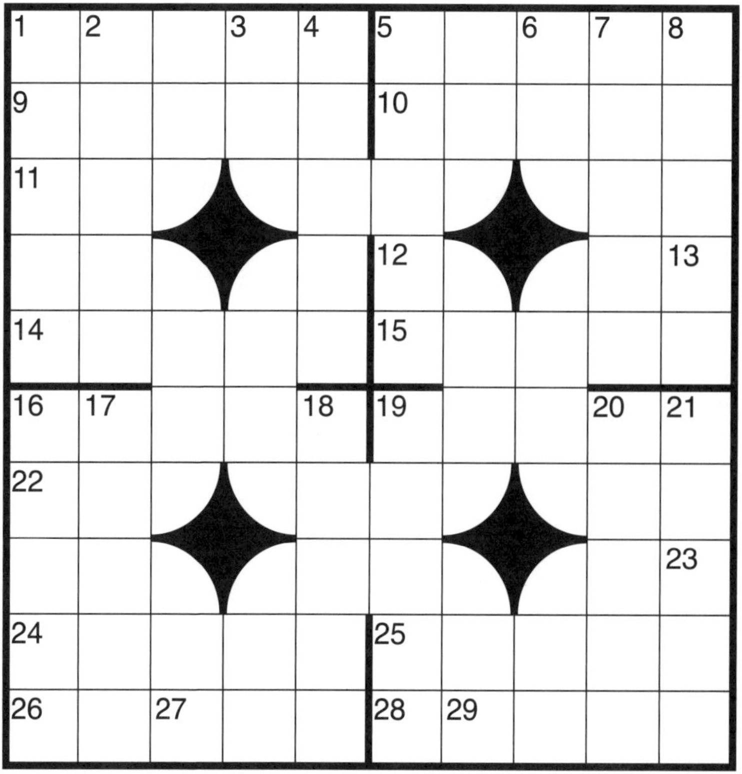
1 2 3 4 5 6 7 8
9 10
11
12 13
14 15
16 17 18 19 20 21
22
23
24 25
26 27 28 29

ROUND THE BEND 3

ACROSS

1 Made like a mole
5 Gilmore of basketball
9 Supercharger type
10 Garner's dad on *The Rockford Files*
14 "Spaghetti western" scorer Morricone
15 March VIP
16 Thickset
19 Asparagus serving
24 DKNY designer
25 Elbow
26 Burma-Shave trademarks
28 Windsor, Ontario's county

DOWN

1 Be quite conspicuous
2 Charade: Hyph.
4 "Tiny Bubbles" crooner: 2 wds.
5 Furthers felons
7 Von Bulow portrayer
8 Part of the UAR
16 Defrauds
17 Ex-premier Zhou
18 Sea dog's repertoire
19 Clapboard datum
20 Saw
21 Watchword?

BENT

3 *A Christmas Carol* name
6 "Danny Boy" singer, often
11 Videogame name
12 Pet store purchase: 2 wds.
13 Snide suggestion
22 Patent holder
23 Splashes down
27 Interrogate
29 A famous high jumper

HELTER-SKELTER 1

CLUES

1 Website address start
2 Receptionist, e.g.
3 Wireless inventor
4 Without much wiggle room
5 Wile E. Coyote's supplier
6 Mouse-spotting cry
7 Act obsequiously
8 One of Chekhov's *Three Sisters* sisters
9 Viticulturist's concern
10 *The Scarlet Letter* heroine
11 C.S. Lewis kiddie-lit locale
12 Replies
13 Hourglass fill
14 Victorious admiral at Manila Bay
15 Cowardly
16 Perry Mason's field
17 City in Uttar Pradesh
18 Bacterium
19 BLT spread
20 Jason's craft

21 *Children of a Lesser* ___
22 "Heavens to Betsy!": 2 wds.
23 They cost $200 each in Monopoly: Abbr.
24 Ride a windjammer
25 Cover
26 Sort

1	2				16		15
8			21		22	17	
		19			18	11	
		9	20				
		23			5		14
7	3					4	26
		10		24			25
		6		13		12	

HELTER-SKELTER 2

CLUES

1 Comic strip that inspired a Broadway musical
2 Alabama university
3 Kentucky Derby wreath
4 Day of rest
5 Basic unit of computer information
6 Wrenching experience
7 Thick mass of hair
8 The James gang, e.g.
9 Desk accessory
10 Wild duck
11 ___ Moore (Hormel brand)
12 Compositor's selections
13 Home base of Nordstrom, Inc.
14 *Wind in the Willows* character
15 1971 Spielberg TV movie
16 Extreme
17 Deli loaf
18 88 days, on Mercury
19 Performance
20 Exclaim
21 Fred Gipson's "Old" mutt
22 Always, in verse
23 Encouraging word?
24 Oppression
25 ___ "The Man" Musial

24		22				21	11
			18		19		
23	16			17		20	
15			14		7	3	12
25			9			8	
			5			4	
	10						
1		2			6		13

HELTER-SKELTER 3

CLUES

1 Billfold
2 Inamorata
3 Samuel Butler's utopian satire
4 1955 Platters hit covered by Ringo 20 years later: 2 wds.
5 Nikkei factor
6 '60s jacket eponym
7 Beverage invented by pharmacist Charles Hires: 2 wds.
8 Life science
9 Sharp tug
10 He dove into Whitewater and came up empty: 2 wds.
11 Long, tiring trip
12 Perrier rival
13 Length × width × depth
14 Fruit tree considered sacred in India
15 Job application datum
16 Where thread goes through

17 Auto named for its country of origin
18 Run up the phone bill
19 Eastern tree, often with widespread branches
20 Parisian pal
21 Pianist/conductor José
22 Furrow
23 Saxophone range
24 Not so safe
25 One of the Trinity

10			9		20	19	
	4			15		14	16
				18		17	21
	1			2		23	6
11							
		13		22	5		
	3	12	8				7
				25		24	

ANSWERS

LANGUAGE PUZZLES

Switchcraft, page 18

1. A COLLEGE education shows a man how LITTLE other people know.
2. The first essential for a PRIME minister is to be a GOOD butcher.
3. Lies are the MORTAR that bind the savage INDIVIDUAL man into the social masonry.
4. Envy DESIRES not so much its own happiness as ANOTHER'S misery.
5. I'm the candidate who forgot to take off her HAT before she threw it in the RING.
6. What we call law and ORDER is machinery for robbing the poor under LEGAL forms.
7. She's the SORT of woman who lives for others—you can always tell the others by their hunted EXPRESSION.
8. It is not ENOUGH to succeed. OTHERS must fail.
9. I know I am among CIVILIZED men because they are FIGHTING so savagely.
10. It is only the WARLIKE power of a civilized people that can give peace to the WORLD.
11. GOVERNMENT is like a baby: an alimentary canal with a big APPETITE at one end and no sense of responsibility at the other.
12. I OWE much; I have nothing; the rest I LEAVE to the poor.

13. The MIND of a bigot is like the pupil of the eye; the more light you pour upon it, the more it will CONTRACT.

14. Nothing is ILLEGAL if a hundred businessmen decide to do it, and that's TRUE anywhere in the world.

15. Democracy gives every MAN the right to be his own OPPRESSOR.

16. She's DESCENDED from a long line her mother LISTENED to.

17. FINANCIAL genius consists almost entirely of avarice and a RISING market.

18. Let your children GO if you WANT to keep them.

Schooner Spool, page 21

1. I wonder how far MOSES would have gone if he had taken a POLL in Egypt.

2. HOW COME there's only one Monopolies Commission?

3. If GOD had CABLE, we're the 24-hour doofus network.

4. I remember things the WAY they SHOULD have been.

5. My own business BORES me to DEATH; I prefer other people's.

6. While he was no DUMBER than an ox, he was NOT any smarter. (Remember, NUMBER can be pronounced with or without the B sound.)

7. She MAY very well pass for forty-three, in the dusk with a LIGHT behind her.

8. If I KNEW myself, I'd RUN away.

9. I got a LOT of ideas. Trouble is, most of them SUCK.

10. A fan club is a group of people who TELL an actor he's not alone in the way he FEELS about himself.

11. SEX is like MONEY; only too much is enough.
12. Our life SEEMS like a trial RUN.
13. Thank heavens we don't GET all the government we PAY for.
14. DID you ever have the MEASLES, and, if so, how many?
15. I was so ugly WHEN I was BORN, the doctor slapped my mother.
16. A sharp tongue is the only TOOL that GROWS keener with constant use.
17. For me the cinema is NOT a slice of life but a PIECE of cake.
18. Blessed are the YOUNG, for they shall inherit the national DEBT.
19. I hate television. I HATE it as much as peanuts. But I can't STOP eating peanuts.
20. The WORST egoist is the person to whom the thought has never occurred that HE might be one.
21. Speed will TURN YOU into your parents.
22. Law practice is the exact opposite of SEX. Even when it's good, it's BAD.
23. The less you BET, the more you LOSE when you win.
24. We often stand in NEED of HEARING what we know full well.
25. We are never so certain of our knowledge as when we're DEAD WRONG.
26. Literature is NEWS that STAYS news.
27. FOR those who know how to read, I have PAINTED my auto-biography.
28. FEW GREAT men could pass Personnel.
29. When you come to a FORK in the road, TAKE it.
30. I do most of my WORK sitting down. That's where I SHINE.

Exchanging Letters, page 26

1. WATER TAKEN in moderation cannot hurt anybody.
2. For the most part, colleges ARE places where pebbles are polished and diamonds are DIMMED.
3. LIFE is MADE up of sobs, sniffles, and smiles, with sniffles predominating.
4. I would have made a terrible PARENT. The first TIME my child didn't do what I wanted, I'd kill him.
5. Babies ARE such a nice way to START people.
6. COUGHING in the THEATER is not a respiratory ailment. It is a criticism.
7. About as big AS the small end of NOTHING whittled to a point.
8. If you have always DONE IT that way, it is probably wrong.
9. GOD may forgive your SINS, but your nervous system won't.
10. I'm now at the age where I've got to PROVE that I'm as GOOD as I never was.
11. When a thing is funny, search it FOR a hidden TRUTH.
12. MONEY IS paper blood.
13. Fall is my favorite season in Los Angeles, watching the birds CHANGE COLOR and fall from the trees.
14. Fame usually COMES to THOSE who are thinking of something else.
15. A NICE MAN is a man of nasty ideas.
16. Large, NAKED, RAW carrots are acceptable as food only to those who live in hutches eagerly awaiting Easter.
17. When I hear a man preach, I like to see him act as if he were FIGHTING BEES.
18. My formula for success? RISE early, WORK late, strike oil.

19. Opera is WHEN a guy gets stabbed in the back and, instead of BLEEDING, he sings.
20. The physician can bury HIS mistakes, but the architect can only advise his client to PLANT vines.
21. He gave HER a look you could have poured on a WAFFLE.
22. I KEEP reading between the LIES.
23. The trouble with opportunity is that it always COMES disguised as hard WORK.
24. FOOLS are only laughed at; WITS are hated.
25. MOST women are not as young as they're PAINTED.

1. An ATHEIST is a guy who watches a Notre Dame–SMU GAME and doesn't CARE who WINS.
2. If I WANTED LIFE to be easy, I should have BEEN BORN in a different universe.
3. A man who takes half a PAGE to say what can be SAID in a sentence WILL be DAMNED.
4. You CAN DO everything with bayonets, SIRE, except SIT on them.
5. TAKE care of the SENSE, and the SOUNDS will take CARE of themselves.
6. A lawyer with his briefcase can STEAL MORE than a hundred MEN with GUNS.

Reunited States, page 31
Puzzle A
1–2. I worry incessantly that I might be too clear.
2–3. I launched the phrase "the war to end war"—and that was not the least of my crimes.

3–1. I read the book of Job last night. I don't think God comes well out of it.

Puzzle B

1–4. Where do we catch the boat for Plato's Republic?

2–1. Instant gratification takes too long.

3–2. You can stroke people with words.

4–3. Ambition is best not naked.

Puzzle C

1–5. You can't build a reputation on what you're going to do.

2–4. Of all sexual aberrations, chastity is the strangest.

3–2. Loneliness is so widespread that it has become, paradoxically, a shared experience.

4–3. Only little states are virtuous.

5–1. I prefer rogues to imbeciles because they sometimes take a rest.

Puzzle D

1–4. A merry Christmas to all my friends except two.

2–5. People say law but they mean wealth.

3–6. If pregnancy were a book, they'd cut out the last two chapters.

4–1. California: the west coast of Iowa.

5–3. I love Mickey Mouse more than any woman I've ever known.

6–2. All diplomacy is a continuation of war by other means.

Puzzle E

1–5. The man who laughs simply has not heard the terrible news.

2–7. Yesterday makes me tired.

3–4. If you can't convince them, confuse them.

4–6. Nationalism is power hunger tempered by self-deception.

5–1. It's a sure sign of summer if the chair gets up when you do.

6–3. Nobody ever fielded 1000 if they tried for the hard ones.

7–2. The past is a bucket of ashes.

Puzzle F

1–4. We believe, first and foremost, what makes us feel that we are fine fellows.

2–7. News expands to fill the time and space allocated to its coverage.

3–5. Heaven for climate, hell for society.

4–8. The only time people dislike gossip is when it's about them.

5–2. History is what bitter old men write.

6–3. I've got no axiom to grind.

7–1. His ignorance is encyclopedic.

8–6. I've actually had people come up to me and ask me to autograph their guns.

Sum Fun, page 35

1. Jealousy is the tribute mediocrity pays to genius.

2. History makes one shudder and laugh by turns.

3. They shoot too many pictures and not enough actors.

4. Managing is getting paid for home runs someone else hits.

5. Last week I went to Philadelphia but it was closed.

6. A sincere diplomat is like dry water or wooden iron.

7. It was simple and beautiful as all truly great swindles are.

8. We hate those faults most in others which we are guilty of ourselves.

9. Official history is a matter of believing murderers on their own word.

10. Henry James was one of the nicest old ladies I ever met.

11. Money couldn't buy friends, but you got a better class of enemy.
12. Everybody gets so much information all day long that they lose their common sense.
13. Man is a creature who lives not upon bread alone, but principally by catchwords.
14. The profession of book writing makes horse racing seem like a solid, stable business.
15. Self-righteousness is a loud din raised to drown the voice of guilt within us.
16. Satire is a sort of glass, wherein beholders do generally discover everybody's face but their own.
17. Hanging is too good for a man who makes puns; he should be drawn and quoted.

Order in the Quote, page 41

1. A GUILTY CONSCIENCE is the MOTHER OF INVENTION.
2. I think there IS a WORLD MARKET for MAYBE FIVE COMPUTERS.
3. There are AMIABLE VICES and OBNOXIOUS VIRTUES.
4. Don't JUST DO SOMETHING, STAND THERE.
5. We are not AT WAR WITH EGYPT. We are in an ARMED CONFLICT.
6. CANNED MUSIC is like AUDIBLE WALLPAPER.
7. With TWICE AS MUCH BRAIN, he'd still BE A HALF-WIT.
8. WASHINGTON IS a city of NORTHERN CHARM and SOUTHERN EFFICIENCY.
9. A LITTLE INACCURACY SOMETIMES SAVES TONS OF EXPLANATION.

Drop a Line, page 44

1. Moderation is a virtue only in those who are thought to have a choice.
2. An original thinker is the person who is the first to steal an idea.
3. To know how many are envious of you, count your admirers.
4. A poor relation is the most irrelevant thing in nature.
5. Mediocre minds usually dismiss anything beyond their understanding.
6. Having been unpopular in high school is not just cause for book publication.
7. There are no right answers to wrong questions.

Excess Baggage, page 46

1. Good pitching will always stop good hitting and VICE-VERSA.
2. MIRACLES do happen, but one has to work very hard for them.
3. Acting is merely the art of keeping a large group of people FROM COUGHING.
4. Nothing is real unless it happens on TELEVISION.
5. Quarrels would not last long if the fault were ON ONE SIDE ONLY.
6. God will forgive me—that's HIS BUSINESS!
7. A wise woman will always let her husband HAVE HER WAY.

Suspended Sentences, page 48

1. Never argue with a man whose job depends on not being convinced.

2. Life has to be given a meaning because of the obvious fact that it has no meaning.
3. Old age puts more wrinkles in our minds than on our faces.
4. If triangles had made a god, it would have three sides.
5. The secret of respectability is to ignore what you don't understand.
6. One day's exposure to mountains is better than cartloads of books.
7. Man is the leopard who knows how to change his spots.
8. Trends, like horses, are easier to ride in the direction they are already going.
9. Doctors will have more lives to answer for in the next world than even we generals.
10. The test of a real comedian is whether you laugh at him before he opens his mouth.

Halving It All, page 51
1. Economic forecasters exist to make astrologers look good.
2. Humor is just another defense against the universe.
3. Failure is the condiment that gives success its flavor.
4. What the country needs is dirtier fingernails and cleaner minds.
5. Our honesty is as much the effect of interest as principle.
6. Laugh and the world laughs with you, snore and you sleep alone.
7. It is an interesting question how far men would retain their relative rank if they were divested of their clothes.
8. The appellation of heretics has always been applied to the less numerous party.

9. If Moses were to go up Mt. Sinai today, the two tablets he'd bring down would be aspirin and Prozac.

10. Like many businessmen of genius he learned that free competition was wasteful, monopoly efficient.

11. Every day people are straying away from the church and going back to God.

12. Pollution of language spreads everywhere, like great globs of sludge crowding the shore of public thought.

13. The first rule of democracy is to distrust all leaders who begin to believe their own publicity.

14. Most people work just hard enough not to get fired and get paid just enough money not to quit.

15. Venice is like eating an entire box of chocolate liqueurs at one go.

Mixed Signals, page 63

1. a. No victor believes in chance.
   b. Woman was God's second mistake.
2. a. I am in my anecdotage.
   b. No good deed goes unpunished.
3. a. Newspapers should be limited to advertising.
   b. Rascality has limits, stupidity has not.
4. a. It's easier to be critical than correct.
   b. A conservative government is an organized hypocrisy.
5. a. Coffee is not my cup of tea.
   b. We're overpaying him, but he's worth it.
6 a. Promises and pie crust are made to be broken.
   b. May you live all the days of your life.
7. a. Old and young, we are all on our last cruise.

b. I regard you with an indifference closely bordering on aversion.
8. a. That politician tops his part/Who readily can lie with art.
   b. Those who in quarrels interpose/Must often wipe a bloody nose.

Mixed Doubles, page 66

1. a. Parents are the bones on which children sharpen their teeth.
   b. If Botticelli were alive today, he'd be working for Vogue.
2. a. Lawyers spend a great deal of their time shoveling smoke.
   b. If a man is a minority of one, we lock him up.
3. a. It is wonderful to be here in the great state of Chicago.
   b. Republicans understand the importance of bondage between a mother and child.
4. a. Whenever a friend succeeds, a little something in me dies.
   b. Reality is something the human race doesn't handle very well.
5. a. Sometimes I feel like a figment of my own imagination.
   b. If love is the answer, could you rephrase the question?
6. a. Early to bed, early to rise, work like hell, and advertise.
   b. If I only had a little humility, I would be perfect.

Exchanging Words, page 69

1. a. Modern poets add a lot of water TO THEIR INK.
   b. When ideas fail, words come IN VERY HANDY.
2. a. Politics are too serious a matter to be left to THE POLITICIANS.
   b. The better I get to know men, the more I find myself LOVING DOGS.

3. a. What small potatoes we all are, compared with WHAT WE MIGHT BE!
   b. The effect of talk on any subject is to STRENGTHEN ONE'S OWN OPINION.
4. a. All this fuss about sleeping together. For physical pleasure I'd sooner go to my DENTIST ANY DAY.
   b. We cherish our friends not for their ability to amuse us, but for ours TO AMUSE THEM.
5. a. In heaven an angel is NOBODY IN PARTICULAR.
   b. Self-sacrifice enables us to sacrifice OTHERS WITHOUT BLUSHING.
6. a. Never try to lick ice cream off A HOT SIDEWALK!
   b. No problem is too big to RUN AWAY FROM.
7. a. Speech was given to man to CONCEAL HIS THOUGHTS.
   b. To avoid being called a flirt, she ALWAYS YIELDED EASILY.
8 a. In Maine they have not a summer BUT A THAW.
   b. That which we call sin in others, is EXPERIMENT FOR US.

Two-Sums, page 72

1. He who hesitates is a damned fool.
   You're never too old to grow younger.
2. Californians are not without their faults.
   Creditors have better memories than debtors.
3. Humor is emotional chaos remembered in tranquility.
   Seeing is deceiving. It's eating that's believing.
4. (I) don't think being funny is anyone's first choice.
   Is sex dirty? Only if it's done right.
5. (You) can't teach an old dogma new tricks.
   She wore a low but futile decolletage.

6. Every exit is an entrance somewhere else.
   Imagination without skill gives us modern art.
7. Guilt: the gift that keeps on giving.
   Housework can kill you if done right.
8. Religious tolerance is a kind of infidelity.
   Where there's a will, there's a won't.
9. It's better to be looked over than overlooked.
   To err is human, but it feels divine.
10. Divorces are made in heaven.
    Only the shallow know themselves.
11. All styles are good, except the tiresome kind.
    England has 42 religions and only two sauces.
12. City life: millions of people being lonesome together.
    I have traveled a good deal in Concord.
13. Poetry is the bill and coo of sex.
    Truth lies at the end of a circle.
14. (The) statesman shears the sheep, the politician skins them.
    Every April God rewrites the Book of Genesis.
15. Art is the sex of the imagination.
    I drink to make other people interesting.

Disappairing Acts, page 80

1. a. How do we know that the people we meet are not
      computers programmed to simulate people?
   b. The most important fact about Spaceship Earth: an
      instruction book didn't come with it.
2. a. Fight fair but don't forget the other lad may not know
      where the belt line is.

   b. To most people a savage nation is one that doesn't wear uncomfortable clothes.

3. a. Gluttony is an emotional escape, a sign that something is eating us.

   b. We must love one another, but nothing says we have to like each other.

4. a. It has long been an axiom of mine that the little things are infinitely the most important.

   b. Mediocrity knows nothing higher than itself, but talent instantly recognizes genius.

5. a. An appeaser is one who feeds a crocodile—hoping it will eat him last.

   b. It was one of those events which are incredible until they happen.

6. a. The only way of catching a train, I've discovered, is to miss the train before.

   b. To be clever enough to get all that money, one must be stupid enough to want it.

7. a. Every day I beat my own previous record for number of consecutive days I've stayed alive.

   b. In labor news, longshoremen walked off the piers today; rescue operations are continuing.

8. a. Autobiography is only to be trusted when it reveals something disgraceful.

   b. England resembles a family, a family with the wrong members in control.

9. a. Promise, large promise, is the soul of an advertisement.

   b. Marriage has many pains but celibacy has no pleasures.

Little Boxes, page 89

1. An actor is not quite a human being—but then, who is?

2. Liberty is the only thing you cannot have unless you give it to others.

3. My mother used to get up at 5 A.M. no matter what time it was.

4. To never see a fool, you lock yourself in your room and smash the looking glass.

5. My first wife divorced me on grounds of incompatibility, and besides, I think she hated me.

6. The future is something which everyone reaches at the rate of sixty minutes an hour, whatever he does, whoever he is.

7. I went on a diet, swore off drinking and heavy eating, and in fourteen days I lost two weeks.

8. Freedom of the press is to the machinery of the state what the safety valve is to the steam engine.

9. Compassion is not measured by how many people are on food stamps.

10. I've just got to stop putting things off, starting first thing tomorrow.

11. He was a cock who thought the sun had risen to hear him crow.

12. After coming in contact with a religious man, I always have to wash my hands.

13. There is a time for departure even when there's no certain place to go.

14. It's hard to beat a day in which you are permitted the luxury of four sunsets.

15. Education is the ability to listen to almost anything without losing your temper or your self-confidence.

Thinking Outside the Box, page 93

1. Tonight's forecast: dark. Continuing dark throughout the night and turning widely scattered light in the morning.
2. Most people repent of their sins by thanking God they ain't so wicked as their neighbors.
3. The length of a film should be directly related to the endurance of the human bladder.
4. The reason grandparents and grandchildren get along so well is that they have a common enemy.
5. I don't give a damn for a man that can spell a word only one way.
6. Why should I expect to be exempt from censure, the unfailing lot of an elevated station?
7. Only when one has lost all curiosity has one reached the age to write an autobiography.
8. Old age is ready to undertake tasks that youth shirked because they would take too long.
9. The battle is sometimes to the small, for the bigger they are the harder they fall.
10. Criticizing a political satirist for being unfair is like criticizing a nose guard for being physical.
11. Modesty is the art of encouraging people to find out for themselves how wonderful you are.
12. The Puritan's idea of Hell is a place where everybody has to mind his own business.

13. The most serious charge which can be brought against New England is not Puritanism but February.

14. The lunches of 57 years had caused his chest to slip down into the mezzanine floor.

15. Of all the griefs that harass the distressed,/Sure the most bitter is a scornful jest.

16. It would be very glamorous to be reincarnated as a giant ring on Elizabeth Taylor's finger.

17. When we resist our passions, it is more on account of their weaknesses than our strength.

18. I figure you have the same chance of winning the lottery whether you play or not.

19. Just because your voice reaches halfway around the world doesn't mean you are wiser than when it reached only to the end of the bar.

Few and Far Between, page 100

1. The best things in life aren't things.

2. No man is a hypocrite in his pleasures.

3. Experience is the name everyone gives to their mistakes.

4. I can't afford to waste my time making money.

5. For parlor use, the vague generality is a lifesaver.

6. A liberal will hang you from a lower branch.

7. Many people despise money, but few hurry to give it away.

8. Love is the strangest bird/that ever winged about the world.

9. Show me a hero, and I will write you a tragedy.

10. Any fool can criticize, condemn, and complain—and most fools do.

11. An idealist is a person who helps other people to be prosperous.
12. To have news value is to have a tin can tied to one's tail.
13. My wife is a light eater: as soon as it's light, she starts eating.
14. I have yet to hear a man ask for advice on how to combine marriage and a career.
15. I should not talk so much about myself if there were anybody else whom I knew as well.

Words of a Feather, page 104

1. Those in power codify their privileges into laws.
2. Only good girls keep diaries. Bad girls don't have the time.
3. The secret to creativity is knowing how to hide your sources.
4. The painter should not paint what he sees, but what should be seen.
5. I do not regard a broker as a member of the human race.
6. There comes a time in every man's life, and I've had many of them.
7. The great tragedy of Science—the slaying of a beautiful hypothesis by an ugly fact.

Authorized Quotes, page 107

1. How large an income is thrift. CICERO
2. An absurdity is not an obstacle in politics. NAPOLEON
3. You haven't lived until you've died in California. MORT SAHL
4. The stock market has spoiled more appetites than bad cooking. WILL ROGERS

5. Writing free verse is like playing tennis with the net down. ROBERT FROST

6. Ask your child what he wants for dinner only if he's buying. FRAN LEBOWITZ

7. When learning and wisdom hitch up together, they are a bully team. JOSH BILLINGS

8. There's always something suspect about an intellectual on the winning side. VACLAV HAVEL

9. I paint objects as I think them, not as I see them. PABLO PICASSO

10. Do you think God gets stoned? I think so—look at the platypus! ROBIN WILLIAMS

11. We are so fond of each other because our ailments are the same. JONATHAN SWIFT

12. A "gaffe" occurs not when a politician lies, but when he tells the truth. MICHAEL KINSLEY

13. Patriots always talk of dying for their country, and never of killing for their country. BERTRAND RUSSELL

Famous Last Words, page 111

1. Health food makes me SICK.
2. Everything seems stupid when it FAILS.
3. Moral indignation is jealousy with A HALO.
4. Trash has given us an appetite FOR ART.
5. When elephants fight it's the grass that SUFFERS.
6. A man by himself is in bad COMPANY.
7. If you want a friend in Washington, GET A DOG.
8. Unbidden guests are often welcomest when they ARE GONE.
9. The first requirement of a statesman is that HE BE DULL.

10. Freud was the father of psychoanalysis. It had NO MOTHER.

11. A thing is not necessarily true because a man DIES FOR IT.

12. Some of my best leading men have been dogs AND HORSES.

13. You must not blame me if I talk to THE CLOUDS.

14. My forefathers didn't come over on the Mayflower, but they MET THE BOAT.

15. Contrary to popular belief, English women do not wear tweed NIGHTGOWNS.

16. The United States has to move very fast to even STAND STILL.

17. Middle age is when it takes longer to rest than TO GET TIRED.

18. There's no money in poetry, but then there's no poetry in MONEY EITHER.

19. What other culture could have produced someone like Hemingway and not SEEN THE JOKE?

20. When you become used to never being alone, you may consider yourself AMERICANIZED.

21. The book written against fame and learning has the author's name on THE TITLE PAGE.

22. There are times when parenthood seems like nothing but feeding the mouth THAT BITES YOU.

23. I happen to know quite a bit about the South. Spent twenty years THERE ONE NIGHT.

24. If words were invented to conceal thought, newspapers are a great improvement on A BAD INVENTION.

GRID PUZZLES

Missing Links 1 (Page 124)

C	R	I	B	S		B	E	T
A			O					U
R		P	A	L	A	T	E	S
O	P	E	R	A		A		S
U		A	D	D	E	R		L
S	I	R		L	A	P	S	E
E	C	L	A	I	R		H	
S	O	Y		N			E	
	N		A	G	E	N	D	A

Missing Links 2 (Page 125)

M	A	S	T	H	E	A	D	
A	N	Y			D		A	M
G		N			G		I	
E	X	T	E	R	I	O	R	S
N		A			N		Y	
T	A	X	I	D	E	R	M	Y
A	M	E	N		S		A	
S	I	S		U	S	I	N	G
	D					F		O

Missing Links 3 (Page 126)

F	I	R	E	S	I	D	E
A	N			**C**	E		
I	**N**	**F**	R	A	R	E	**D**
R			**L**	**A**	P		
W	**A**	**F**	**F**	**L**	**I**	**N**	**G**
A			L	I	N	E	
Y	A	H	O	O		**S**	
S			E	N	D	S	

Missing Links 4 (Page 127)

O	V	E	R	S	E	**A**	S
P	**I**	G		A		P	I
A	**D**	O	P	T	I	O	N
L	E	T		**I**		S	
S	**O**	I	**L**	**S**		T	
		S	**O**	**F**	**T**	**L**	**Y**
O		T	O	Y		**E**	
H	A	S	**P**				

Missing Links 5 (Page 128)

A	C	C	U	R	A	C	Y
D		O			D	O	E
A	P	R	I	C	O	T	
M	A	P		H		E	X
A		O	A	R		R	
N	A	R	C	O	T	I	C
T		A	I	M		E	
	E	L	D	E	R	S	

Missing Links 6 (Page 129)

M	O	T	O	R	B	U	S
A	D	O			E		C
Y	O	N			L		O
O	M	I	S	S	I	O	N
R	E	C	I	P	E		E
	T		R	A	V	E	S
R	E	C	E	D	E		
	R		N	E	R	V	Y

Missing Links 7 (Page 130)

M	A	C	H	E	T	E	
A	D		E			Y	E
C	O	U	R	A	G	E	
R			O		A	S	P
A		H	I		T	O	O
M	E	A	N	D	E	R	S
E		L	E	A	S	E	S
	N	O	S	Y			E

Missing Links 8 (Page 131)

B	A	T	H	R	O	B	E
	S	H	E			A	
	E	A	R	M	A	R	K
P	A	N	E			K	
L		E	S	T	E	E	M
U	P		Y	O	K	E	
M	E			W	E	P	T
	G	R	I	N	D		O

Boomerangs 1 (Page 132)

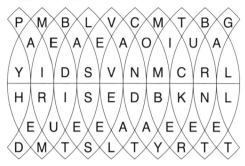

Boomerangs 2 (Page 134)

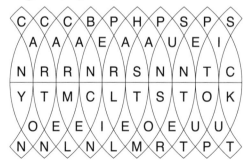

Boomerangs 3 (Page 136)

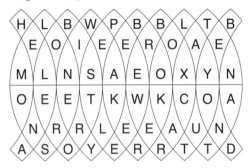

Boomerangs 4 (Page 138)

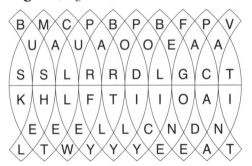

Boomerangs 5 (Page 140)

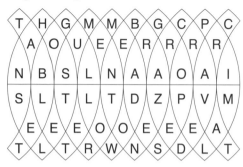

Boomerangs 6 (Page 142)

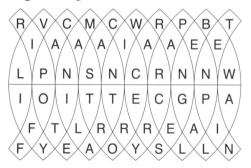

Boomerangs 7 (Page 144)

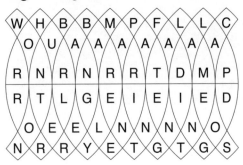

Boomerangs 8 (Page 146)

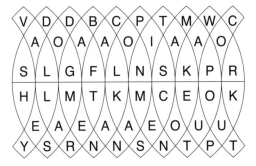

Cross Anagrams 1 (Page 148)
DARNER, CINEMA, GLEANS, KITSCH, TONIER, DETAIL;
ERRAND, ANEMIC, ANGELS, SHTICK, ORIENT, DILATE

Cross Anagrams 2 (Page 150)
ELAPSE, BADGER, RASPED, FASTER, ELUDED, METEOR;
PLEASE, BARGED, SPREAD, STRAFE, DELUDE, REMOTE

Cross Anagrams 3 (Page 152)
RIPEST, BEDLAM, ASCOTS, KAYOED, ADHERE, REWARD;
PRIEST, BLAMED, COASTS, OKAYED, HEADER, DRAWER

Cross Anagrams 4 (Page 154)
CANOED, SAMPLE, TARTAN, DISBAR, PARSON, MARGIN;
DEACON, MAPLES, RATTAN, BRAIDS, APRONS, ARMING

Cross Anagrams 5 (Page 156)
PLEBES, TENURE, STATIC, CHANTS, RISQUE, COVERT;
BLEEPS, TUREEN, ATTICS, SNATCH, QUIRES, VECTOR

Cross Anagrams 6 (Page 158)
FOREST, KISSER, REGARD, SLEUTH, ADVERB, TROUPE;
SOFTER, SKIERS, GRADER, HUSTLE, BRAVED, POUTER

Cross Anagrams 7 (Page 160)
BOSSES, TOPICS, BATHER, PISTON, MEDALS, TRANCE;
OBSESS, OPTICS, BREATH, POINTS, DAMSEL, NECTAR

Cross Anagrams 8 (Page 162)
TROVES, RUSTIC, SINGED, SHINER, RIOTED, TINSEL;
VOTERS, CITRUS, DESIGN, SHRINE, EDITOR, LISTEN

Word Spiral 1 (Page 164)

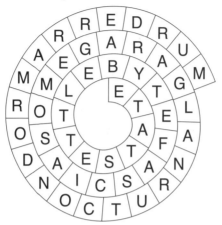

Word Spiral 2 (Page 166)

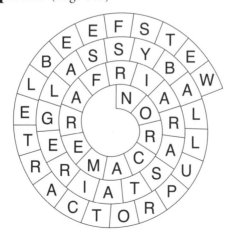

Word Spiral 3 (Page 168)

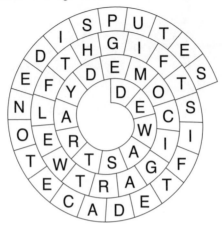

Word Spiral 4 (Page 170)

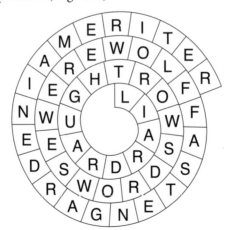

Word Spiral 5 (Page 172)

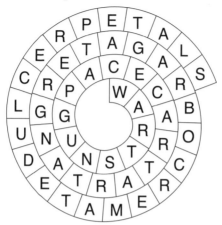

Word Spiral 6 (Page 174)

Word Spiral 7 (Page 176)

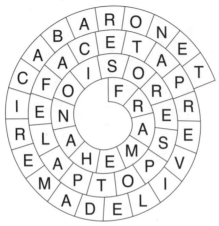

Word Spiral 8 (Page 178)

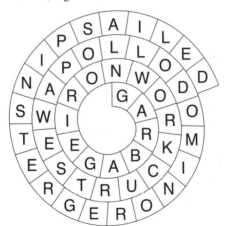

Cross-O 1 (Page 180)
Condiment: ketchup, mustard, onions, pepper, relish

Cross-O 2 (Page 181)
Woodwind: bassoon, clarinet, flute, piccolo

Cross-O 3 (Page 182)
Utensil: colander, funnel, grater, spatula, strainer

Cross-O 4 (Page 183)
Officer: admiral, captain, colonel, general, lieutenant

Cross-O 5 (Page 184)
Fabric: cotton, linen, rayon, tweed

Cross-O 6 (Page 185)
Island: Barbados, Corsica, Cyprus, New Zealand, Sumatra

Cross-O 7 (Page 186)
Carriage: buckboard, cabriolet, hansom, landau, surrey

Cross-O 8 (Page 187)
Horse: Arabian, mustang, palomino, pinto

ANSWERS
Grid Puzzles

Weaving 1 (Page 188)

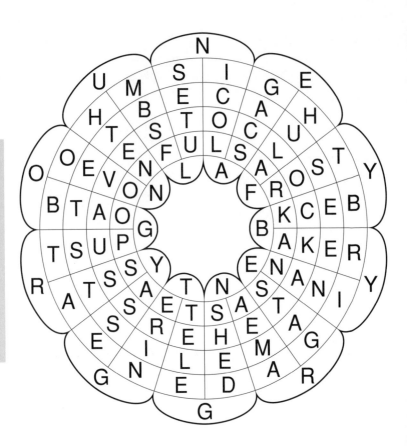

Weaving 2 (Page 190)

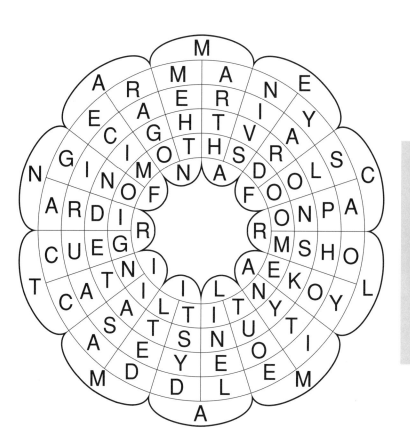

Weaving 3 (Page 192)

Weaving 4 (Page 194)

Quadrants 1 (Page 196)

S	W	A	Y	Z	E	N	A	S	C	A	R
P	O	P	L	A	R	S	V	E	L	T	E
A	M	A	N	D	A	R	E	C	A	L	L
R	B	C	R	O	M	A	N	S	R	A	A
S	A	H	A	R	A	C	U	T	E	S	Y
E	T	E	B	A	R	T	E	R	T	T	S
C	I	S	B	I	K	I	N	I	K	L	U
O	N	T	I	M	E	V	I	V	I	A	N
R	F	A	S	E	R	E	N	E	T	R	I
G	A	R	G	L	E	G	E	C	K	O	S
I	N	V	A	D	E	A	T	E	A	S	E
S	T	E	F	A	N	S	Y	N	T	A	X

Quadrants 2 (Page 198)

S	O	L	E	M	N	T	H	O	R	P	E
H	U	E	V	O	S	M	O	H	A	I	R
A	T	M	O	S	T	A	W	A	K	E	N
B	L	A	M	A	U	L	E	D	I	T	E
B	E	N	O	I	T	A	L	A	N	I	S
Y	T	S	S	C	H	U	L	Z	G	N	T
P	T	O	Q	U	A	R	T	Z	G	Q	A
R	E	T	U	R	N	I	O	L	A	U	S
I	C	O	E	S	T	A	T	E	R	A	S
S	H	O	G	U	N	T	H	I	C	K	E
M	I	L	D	L	Y	M	E	T	I	E	R
S	E	E	S	A	W	D	E	P	A	R	T

Quadrants 3 (Page 200)

P	O	R	T	I	A	L	A	S	S	O	S
A	K	I	M	B	O	E	G	M	O	N	T
P	A	P	I	E	R	A	R	G	U	E	R
A	Y	E	E	R	A	S	E	D	G	W	A
Y	E	S	S	I	R	H	E	E	H	A	W
A	D	T	T	A	O	I	S	T	T	Y	S
S	M	P	A	Q	U	I	N	O	A	N	U
T	A	R	T	A	N	T	E	U	T	O	N
U	L	U	E	N	D	E	A	R	T	R	E
P	I	N	A	T	A	F	R	A	U	D	S
I	C	E	M	A	N	C	L	I	N	I	C
D	E	S	I	S	T	Z	Y	D	E	C	O

Quadrants 4 (Page 202)

N	I	M	I	T	Z	C	H	I	L	L	S
A	R	A	G	O	N	K	A	R	E	E	M
V	O	L	U	M	E	F	R	I	N	G	E
A	N	I	R	A	T	T	L	E	G	R	A
J	O	B	E	T	H	W	A	I	T	E	R
O	N	U	G	O	R	I	N	G	H	E	S
O	G	S	G	R	I	N	C	H	R	J	S
D	A	N	I	E	L	G	O	T	H	A	M
D	L	I	E	L	L	E	R	Y	Y	L	A
J	O	P	L	I	N	P	O	T	T	E	R
O	R	E	L	S	E	A	N	T	H	E	M
B	E	R	T	H	A	W	A	R	M	L	Y

Catching Some Z's 1 (Page 204)

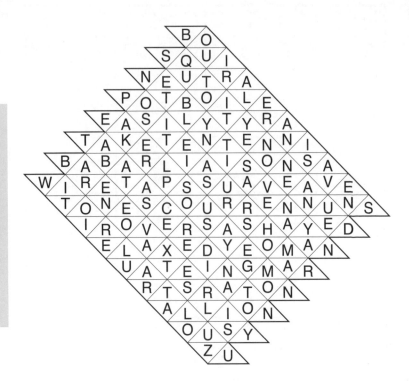

Catching Some Z's 2 (Page 206)

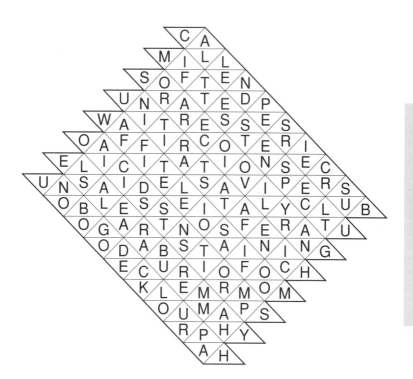

Catching Some Z's 3 (Page 208)

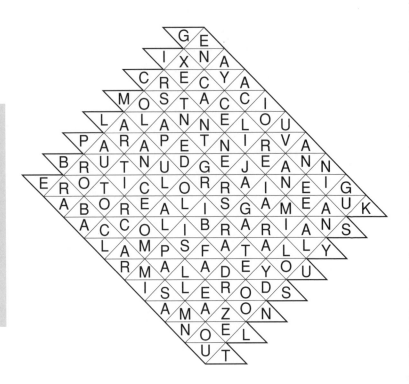

Catching Some Z's 4 (Page 210)

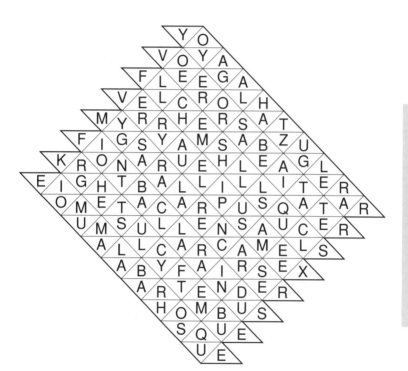

Target Practice 1 (Page 212)

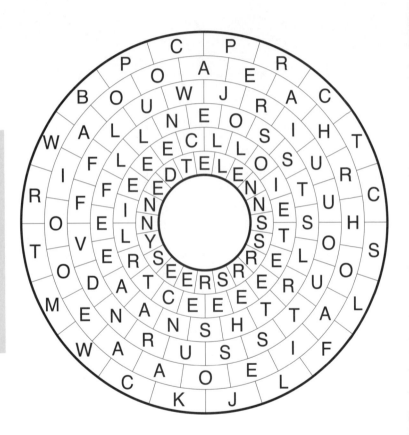

Target Practice 2 (Page 214)

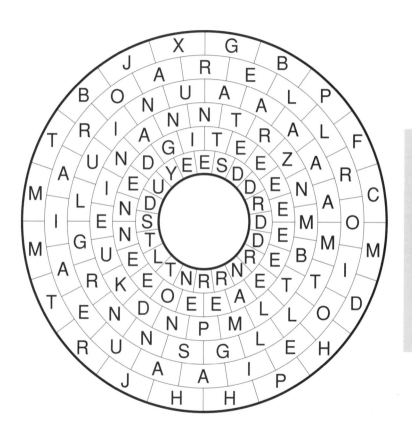

Target Practice 3 (Page 216)

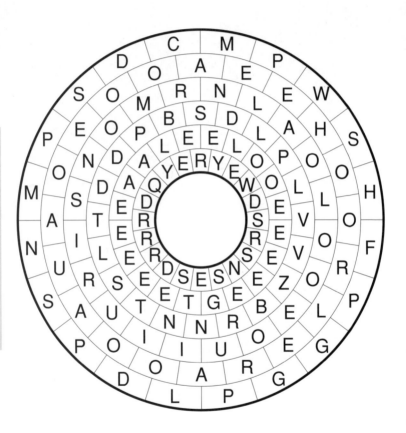

Round the Bend 1 (Page 218)

Round the Bend 2 (Page 220)

Round the Bend 3 (Page 222)

S	P	I	E	D	A	R	T	I	S
T	U	R	B	O	B	E	E	R	Y
A	T	A	E	N	E	Z	N	O	R
R	O	T	S	H	T	R	N	N	I
E	N	N	I	O	S	O	U	S	A
B	E	E	F	Y	S	P	E	A	R
I	N	V	L	A	C	I	N	D	O
L	L	I	M	R	E	P	N	A	L
K	A	R	A	N	N	U	D	G	E
S	I	G	N	S	E	S	S	E	X

Helter-Skelter 1 (Page 224)

W	W	W	O	L	L	E	Y
O	E	O	G	O	D	A	E
T	L	M	R	E	G	N	W
W	C	G	A	R	N	A	E
O	O	R	A	Y	A	R	D
K	M	A	R	C	O	N	I
E	E	P	M	S	A	I	L
S	R	E	W	S	N	A	K

Helter-Skelter 2 (Page 226)

H	R	E	L	L	E	Y	D
A	E	E	Y	E	A	R	I
R	U	L	T	R	A	C	N
D	A	O	T	L	M	R	T
S	W	A	L	T	U	O	Y
H	T	A	B	B	A	S	P
I	M	A	U	I	R	E	E
P	E	A	N	U	T	S	S

Helter-Skelter 3 (Page 228)

K	N	A	Y	N	A	B	E
E	O	O	G	N	A	M	E
N	H	N	O	G	U	Y	I
S	W	A	L	L	E	T	N
T	E	I	O	Y	U	E	E
A	R	V	I	R	Y	N	H
R	E	E	B	T	O	O	R
R	E	I	K	S	I	R	U

INDEX